Taqi M. Albaharna was born in 1930. He is a poet, journalist, and writer. He wrote and published so far ten books, all in Arabic. He was the first Ambassador for Bahrain in Egypt from 1971–1974.

Member of consultative SHURA council, he received five medals of honor.

To my beloved Bahrain

* I love, in Bahrain, my home and neighborhood.
* A face alit with glory and freedom.
* And the voice of a lark chanting on meadowsweet,
* Full of beauty, green, and elegant.
* I also long for beautiful sea shores, where I left my old memories behind.
* And a bend around them and a beautiful road,
* My trustworthy friends, whose sincerity shines like stars deep in my heart.
* I am enchanted with love for my country.

**

Taqi M. Albaharna

A BOY FROM BAHRAIN

Story of a Boy from
Bahrain – 1930-1950

AUSTIN MACAULEY PUBLISHERS™
LONDON • CAMBRIDGE • NEW YORK • SHARJAH

Copyright © Taqi M. Albaharna 2024

The right of Taqi M. Albaharna to be identified as author of this work has been asserted by the author in accordance with Federal Law No. (7) of UAE, Year 2002, Concerning Copyrights and Neighboring Rights.

All rights reserved. No part of this publication may be reproduced, stored in a retrieval system, or transmitted in any form or by any means, electronic, mechanical, photocopying, recording, or otherwise, without the prior permission of the publishers.

Any person who commits any unauthorized act in relation to this publication may be liable to legal prosecution and civil claims for damages.

All of the events in this memoir are true to the best of author's memory. The views expressed in this memoir are solely those of the author.

The age group that matches the content of the books has been classified according to the age classification system issued by the Ministry of Culture and Youth.

ISBN – 9789948775522 – (Paperback)
ISBN – 9789948775539– (E-Book)

Application Number: MC-10-01-4719805
Age Classification: E

Printer Name: iPrint Global Ltd
Printer Address: Witchford, England

First Published 2024
AUSTIN MACAULEY PUBLISHERS FZE
Sharjah Publishing City
P.O Box [519201]
Sharjah, UAE
www.austinmacauley.ae
+971 655 95 202

Good Gesture

*

Written by Professor Ibrahim Al-Arrayed

*

I welcome this good gesture from my pious son, acknowledging that I also wish for an abundance of good for the youthful generation. As I remember the early years of my activity in Bahrain, this polite young man had the perfect image in all the deeds that fill his lifespan—deeds that, from that era and up until today, are shining with all their since that era until today, shining with all their aspects and rich values.

My acquaintance with Taqi Albaharna as a student began, first of all, at the high school that I joined during the Second World War in the forties as a professor sponsored to teach by the Petroleum Concessions Limited Company (PCL). I found in Taqi a young soul thirsty for education and wisdom, wide open to life with a sense of self-satisfaction, which endeavored to combine the means of implementation with the goals to be reached in the broadest ways possible. Taqi's soul does not abandon its objectivity, even in the darkest of plights. It is as if his eye sees what his insight perceives, which makes a connection that overwhelms him with tranquility in all circumstances.

Taqi, when writing about his school days or what followed, does not confine himself to talking about himself only, as others do. Rather, his brush sweeps over the whole painting to showcase the local conditions and the atmosphere of the time period in which the event occurred—an embodiment of the senses in all their dimensions. We live with him in those circumstances that have passed in Bahrain and breathe the air of its suffering that accompanied it again—day or night—as if we are experiencing it again at this very hour.

Every event with Taqi, in addition to being full of description, exceeds its local value when his brush takes charge of his own strokes, so it becomes like a speaking page in the book of the life of humanity, so that you—the reader—touch the essence in a picture that he drew with his pen, so your coexistence with it remains alive, fascinated by how he was able to bring it out within its framework.

Taqi reminds me of his high school days. I find myself at my corner table, living with him there again, and after that, he reminds me of the feeling of the first seminars I attended at the Oruba Club, and I feel myself back again to those glowing moments among the attendees.

It is as if these pages Taqi wrote embody a light for that expressive life that we once lived, as it was, but with an enchanting charm that this artist returned with his brush to create it, and today we all continue to live it with him.

Furthermore, if we reflect on it carefully, it is not limited to us alone or to the history of Bahrain. The impact has risen—with its richness of values—so that every writer worthy of his name abroad who was absent from these circumstances and their atmosphere, back to the beginning, sees how honesty in expression is associated with the beauty that surrounds it from all facets of creating a masterpiece of a painting. This is the characteristic that makes this genius writer unique today among all those whose names have shined in authoring memoirs, whether here or there. According to Taqi, he spoke only about what he saw and never relied on what was relayed on the tongues of others. He had lived, since his childhood, with a rich talent among his people as one of them but with a full awareness of the society's feelings around him and what was hidden in their souls while still retaining his dignity.

I take this opportunity with joy to express to Taqi what I used to feel, in the past and the present, toward every movement he has made. And the last of them to recognize, in addition to the aforementioned memories, is poetry in its true capacity, which has accompanied him, whether organized or scattered, throughout his life. I embrace him as a colleague. May God make his life fruitful for others and a source of always providing those around him with the most delicious fruits.

Ibrahim Al-Arrayed

**

Released on Muharram 10, 1418 AH
Corresponding to May 17, 1997
Bahrain.

= 1 =
Memories of the Flying Wing

*

In the moment that the airplane door is flung open to board an eager line of passengers and each of them makes his way through the crowds to his assigned seat, it is during this brief period of time, which amounts to only minutes, that the passenger's soul encounters a clash between his feelings and tendencies, fueled by instinct, anxiety, and instability, until he finally manages to locate his seat by showing his seat number to the hostess. Those feelings do not dissipate until he seats himself in his designated spot and his hand luggage and necessities are rested in a suitable place next to him, underneath his feet, or overhead. Then, and only then, does the traveler feel a sense of having arranged his transitory abode and a sense of having mentally organized his list of priorities surrounding his journey.

When the traveler fastens his seat belt, his curiosity prompts him to take sideways glances at the people sitting on his right and on his left as he quells his panting breath, trying to establish a relationship between himself and the bustle, clamor, and turbulence that ensues around him.

I, as a traveler, did all of that but without realizing that the passenger seated next to me was strange and abnormal, until he raised his voice, singing in a brazen tone. Passengers turned toward him in astonishment, and even the drink trays trembled in the grasp of the flight hostesses. Their glances then quickly turned to me, which I imagined carried the meaning of a look of pity toward me because of my unfortunate circumstance of having been seated next to him for the flight. Listening to a shrill singing voice is a burden that a person cannot bear, so how about if it occurs in an unfamiliar language like Chinese and the vibrato rings heavily in one's ears?

The singing passenger, who had to be about 60 years old and whose large body seemed to have been crammed forcibly into his seat, intrigued me. He kept reading the same page of a folded newspaper. Then he would scribble something, and you would think he had become completely absorbed in it. But as soon as I made any small movement, he would cease writing and glance at me in a seeming state of self-defense.

He built an imaginary fence around him, complete with imaginary borders. Thus, I came to expect a counterattack each time I made so much as a simple gesture. Had I crossed the line of that invisible border, I imagined him scolding me in a stern tone, "What are you going to do?"

This neighbor encroaching on the freedom of the one sitting beside him reminded me of what has been said on defining the meaning of freedom—that the freedom of one ends where that of the other begins—and I imagined what the human condition would be if each person adhered to what he considers his right, not deviating from it by a hair's breadth. Then it occurred to me what tolerance does to people when the armor of bullying is stripped from them—it protects them from the evil of quarreling unnecessarily, and it saves them from sharpness of speech, harshness of behavior, and fatigue of nerves. I confronted him with a smile and asked him if he was going to Singapore like I was. He replied that he was going to China, then we exited the plane and he disappeared.

A friend in Singapore spoke to me about the society there, as it is a melting pot of origins, races, and sects, many of whom are Chinese, followed by Malaysians, Indians, and small minorities, including some Arab businessmen and Muslims. Our discussion revolved around the question of coexistence and harmony between different nationalities and religions in a single society. I imagine that equilibrium is the key ingredient in Singapore's social, political, economic, and cultural stability. Singaporeans are committed to the existing order out of appreciation for its great achievements in multiple fields.

*

When the state interferes in the affairs of any sect in the service of the common good, it does so in the interest of that sect.

Another friend in Singapore, this one a Muslim, told me that the state imposes a tax of one dollar on the monthly income of every Muslim in order to keep them from needing to resort to foreign donations to build mosques and Islamic institutions. The state used to pay another dollar as a donation. He said that the measure has been so well received that Muslim societies are considering doubling the tax.

The state imposes taxes on individual incomes along with heavy taxes and tariffs on consumer and luxury goods, especially those that are subject to incentive protection, while the rest of the commodities, especially food, are exempt.

One may discover the various means through which the social equilibrium there is maintained. When watching TV, for instance, one can note that its programs air in three different languages: Chinese, Malay, and Hindi, after which the Quran would be recited for Muslims.

Any given visitor may note the absence of social distinctions or feelings of hostility among Singaporeans, despite their great ethnic and religious diversity. He would quickly find that commercial and mutual interests dominate political life—as if the Singaporean is merely a businessman, investor, service provider, and professional, and the rest are customers, the entire country being like a giant commercial store and the state a stern administrative apparatus.

The state is invested in maintaining the political system's social integration, looking after its employees by acknowledging their rights and legitimate aspirations so they can work in peace, and ensuring that the system's foundations not be shaken or devoured.

Singapore is a neighbor to countries that are far larger in size, power, and populations, but they lag behind it in terms of advancement, to varying degrees.

During political elections, the citizens vote in the ruling party and show their support for the government's candidates in the labor union and various other councils, after which political activity ceases and business resumes as usual. The Chinese, whose population in Singapore is high and who, in fact, represent the vast majority of Singaporean immigrants, are content with the cultural and social dimensions of their identity and enjoy good relations with their neighbors. Similarly, the Malaysians also get along well with their neighbors, as they continue to immigrate from Malaysia in search of work, residence, business, as well as for investment opportunities. The same applies to Indians, along with the Muslim and Arab minority, as well.

*

The architect of this unique and ever-vigilant system is the renowned Prime Minister, Lee Kwan Yew, who has become an eternal national symbol, a role model in civility, and an expert in domestic and international politics, as attested by today's prominent world leaders. And when one explores the functions of the office of the Prime Minister, one finds bureaus for combating pollution and administrative corruption, representative of various provinces and electoral administrations. These bureaus are concerned with the affairs of the Council of Ministers, religious affairs, justice and peace, the system of precedence, decorations, the national flag, citizen's advisory committees, and—finally—the Public Utilities Council. Ministers carry out the ministerial duties entrusted to them. Singapore is governed by a democratic parliament and is ruled by the president of the republic.

Henceforth, those notes were what I wrote about Singapore on one of my visits in 1970.

They were originally motivated by the behavior of the Chinese passenger who had started singing on the plane next to me, and it does not imply that I typically jot down notes while traveling, nor does it mean that I am always unlucky in regards to who I am surrounded by while traveling.

On one occasion, years before that, I found myself in the seat next to an American woman while I was traveling to Cedar Rapids. We didn't talk for some time, but I kept peeking at an educational book that she was reading, and perhaps she was peeping also at a paper I was occupying my time with. Then she left the huge book as if she had gotten tired of reading it, so I asked her permission to browse the book. Then I said, "If my hunch is correct, you are a teacher."

And she said, "Yes, school principal. And I don't even need to guess about you, because when I look at your briefcase, I can be sure that you're a businessman."

I had assumed that my answer in the affirmative would impress her or rouse her curiosity, but she shook her head in astonishment and said that the last thing she imagined was that a businessman would be interested in reading a book on education. She then went on to explain her preconceptions about businessmen, saying that, in her opinion, they live in a narrow world, only focusing on matters of money and profits. Literature and culture were on the sidelines of their thinking, according to her. Then she mentioned the paper that I was reading and said it must be reports on commercial deals, but I explained to her that I am not from America and that its provisions do not apply to the environment in which I lived, and that among the merchants and businessmen in our country in the Middle East, a good percentage of them have great interest in culture, literary, and intellectual affairs, and that my ancestors were once the pioneers of literary awakening and the dawn of civilization. As for the paper, which I had been busy reading, it contained verses of poetry. This came as quite a shock to her. She clearly had not expected that, but then she abruptly asked me if I would read an excerpt of the poetry aloud, as it was in Arabic. As I recited the lines of poetry slowly, she was jotting down something in English that I presumed were notes, and as soon as I finished reading, she did not inquire about their meaning, rather the name of the writer.

So, I told her that he was a famous poet from Lebanon who had immigrated to America, whose name is Elia Abu Madhi. She wrote down his name and then said, "I'm going to read the verses in your language, then you'll give me the grade I deserve." I was dumbfounded when I heard her recite the verses from her English notes in the same way as I had read them in Arabic, with the same exact syntax movements, as if she was exploring her childhood past through the transparent meanings of the poetry. Then she asked me to translate the meanings. In my poor English, I translated to her the poetry as follows: *(The poet addresses his homeland, Lebanon).

* Home Land of Stars*

*(Homeland of the stars, I am here. Do you remember who I am?

*If you glimpse in the distant past, you will find a young boy, naïve and astray. That is me.

* Full of joy, frolicking in your fields, humming with the breeze.

Climbing trees without feeling bored or weak.

*He turns to branches, sharpening them like swords or spears.

*And wading into the mud of winter in amusement and joy.

*He does not fear evil eyes nor evil tongues.

*He demonizes himself just for others to say he is a demon.)

*

Then I said, "If it is within you to show such talent, then you truly are a teacher, and if it is a compliment, then it is better than a thousand apologies." Then she left, and I continued my trip, with the verses stuck in my mind and still, I repeat them whenever I turn to the era of my youth and childhood.

*

Certainly, the beauty of nature in Bahrain cannot compare to that of Lebanon. However, nature did not skimp on its beauty in Bahrain either. In the seventeenth century, one of the Portuguese historians wrote about Bahrain, noting that it had three hundred villages, all of which were rich in dates, figs, pomegranates, and peaches, as well as fresh springs. Another historian of that era mentioned pearl diving and highlighted the fact that there were 600 sailing ships in Bahrain. Most of this description was still applicable to Bahrain during the thirties of the last century. When I was a boy, I used to do what the poet Elia Abu Madhi did in his youth, including wading in the winter mud, playing with sticks, humming with the wind, etc. The city of Manama, capital of Bahrain, where I grew up. Manama was embraced in the arms of a fertile crescent, supporting it toward the sea at its southern edge. In fact, Manama itself used to spread among its homes islands of oases and orchards known as "Dalia," as in Dalia of the Kanoo family, the Muayyad family, and Ibn Rajab, next to the famous Al-Baghsha Zoo. While the people of Manama, residing toward the coast, rush to these varicose veins most of the time, greeted by the welcome of their owners, others resort, on their vacations from work, to the fertile gardens and water springs close to Manama. The famous Al-Moomin Mosque was near my house. In front of the mosque, a very small stream of water was known as "al-Mishber." It was 12 inches wide and originated from a natural spring at a nearby police fort. It was used by worshippers to perform ablution before their prayers as well as by housewives, mostly for washing their dirty laundry and dishes.

However, it always seemed that the activities going around the Mosque had not been enough to satisfy the eager hearts of the young boys. Another exciting event would await them on the main roads of Manama.

That was when the parade of police and Bedouin watchmen would start marching in the streets from the police station to the Manama Palace to show their loyalty to the Ruler of Bahrain, His Highness Sheikh Hamad Bin Essa al-Khalifa.

The police march came first, with the policemen riding horses and waving Bahraini national flags, accompanied by the marching band. Next came the Bedouins performing a sort of war dance performed with swords and old guns, which were shot off in the air. They would repeatedly shout out the lyrics to War (Al-Arda) while dancing to them, such as the song lyrics, "I was taught how to use a gun while I was still small."

After the parade passed, the boys would poke fun, trying to imitate the Bedouins. I used to join them, carrying a stick and performing the Arda in a childish way.

The peasants inside the farms themselves would become annoyed at this scene. They did not see it as naïve, childish play but rather the path of demons who deserved to be disciplined. This childish adventure would continue until its end at the natural spring of "Umm Al-Sha'um," passing through the rock of "Umm Humar," i.e., Mother of the Donkey. The children would pay respect to this rock and—like other passers-by—donate some food because they were taught that the Mother of the Donkey would punish naughty boys at midnight, the topic about which many myths were circulated.

The journey back was perpetually characterized by a kind of aggressive attitude against some gardens on their way back home. They felt free to eat any fruits and vegetables on their path to satisfy their hungry little bellies. The famous garden owner, Al-Arrayed, allowed children to eat lettuce, tomatoes, and some fruits for free, but its great owner, Mansour Al-Arrayed, would often scold us and warn us not to do the same on other properties. He specially warned us not to annoy the Indian sect, namely the "Banyan" Indians, who used to wash themselves from the nearby water spring carrying their name, Ein Albanyan, or to follow their funeral processions repeating the dead slogan (Ram Ram Margie).

In the year 1937, I was seven years old and was enrolled in my school, Alkhalifia Primary School for Boys, which was quite near to my house in Manama. I thought I was mature enough to stop playing with street boys and to make friends with my new schoolmates. In the very hot summer months, I used to find relief in walking alone to a nearby garden owned by a famous business friend of my father, Alhaj Hassan Almudaife.

I would sometimes spend the whole day there, enjoying the excitement, resting in the lap of nature. I used to swim in the small pool of fresh water and listen to the singing of the birds. I used to take some fruits home with me. Myself, I have a quiet nature and love quiet resorts. I still, to this day, deliberately choose quiet resorts while traveling abroad.

**

= 2 =
Children of Our Neighborhood

*

The pre-Islamic poet Imru al-Qays described his horse as being well-known for its hit and run.

"Deceit, fleeing, coming, orchestrating together, like a boulder that a torrent smashed from above." He also described the speed of his horse's mobility in catching the hunt by saying:

"So, my horse could reach the front herd and return back to the rest so quickly that it was as if they were tied together in a tight bundle."

*

The students learned about those poems at school, and it may have been difficult for their young minds to understand and imagine the concepts as they really were. As for me, I did not find it difficult to comprehend these strange descriptions and imagine them in nature. The reason for that was: "Abu Abboud," a tall, strong man who had lost his eyesight a long time ago.

Children would poke fun at him, circling him and shouting, "Blind man, blind man!" until he would become annoyed and angry.

In our neighborhood, when young boys—in the midst of their immersion in play—would suddenly feel that the earth was trembling beneath their feet and that a giant human shadow was heading toward them from the west and enveloping them by a cloud, they would realize that the time to disperse was approaching because of the call to prayer. And they would realize that Abu Abboud was coming for the prayer and that it was time to make fun of him.

A sense of panic would spread among the boys, and each of them would take the initiative to gather some of their tools that were scattered on the playing field then to escape from the narrow alley to the wide square near the mosque, as they would realize that Abu Abboud's hurried and bold steps were being led by a long bamboo stick, his eyes closed—which meant that most of them would not give most of them a chance to escape. Soon, the small yard would turn into a field of hit and run. He might have caught one or two of the boys, their legs stumbling toward each other. He was never satisfied with the targets that were available to him, but rather would extend his arm and long stick to reach the rest of the boys who were lining up in front of him in the wide yard to stalk him, then retreat from him as they continued to shout, "Blind man, blind man!" Subconsciously, he had been doing what the horse of Imru al-Qays did in catching the herd.

*

I did not join in the group of those who would flee in front of him, so he would have recognized me as soon as he put the palm of his broad, dry hand on my head and face, sending my heart into a panic. Then he would leave me alone, as if he was convinced—being our next-door neighbor—that I was not really one of them. He would say to me, "My stick is not for you. Return home safely, and leave these impolite children." Despite being blind, he had great insight. He played the role of news reporter, as well as sometimes stepping in to be the "muezzin with," the one who recites the call to prayer.

As for those who would harass him, they would be hit by his long stick. He was able to distinguish each one of them by their voices and would threaten them to complain to their fathers after the prayer in the mosque, which would lead to them being punished at home.

*

This is how each day would pass for the little boys in our neighborhood, full of excitement and full of surprises. They did not have the slightest understanding of the meaning of a quiet, monotonous life, and if they lacked the element of excitement for a while, they would create it amongst themselves by quarreling individually or in groups—one group against another. Housewives in the neighborhood would get annoyed by the boys' noise and their quarrels, so they would throw on their heads from the rooftops—while they were oblivious—the spoiled remains of coffee beans, leftovers of food, or dirty water of any kind. The children would become sad, their handkerchiefs dirtied, and their faces streaming with tears as they ran back home expecting punishment.

Fathers would punish their children using cane sticks, just as my father had done to me. They would count each misdoing with each strike until the little boy shouted repeatedly, "By God, I repent. By God, I repent," crying so profusely that their mothers would interfere to stop the caning of the helpless boys.

Fathers would also punish their adult children for not performing the five daily Muslim prayers.

The tendency of housewives toward the fun and frivolity of boys would differ from one house to another. When the ball was deflected to the roof of a house, some of them would volunteer to retrieve it. If they found acceptance and the door was opened for them to enter, they would add to that another requirement, which would be drinking water. If the tolerance was increased, the boys' steps would slow around the house to satisfy their curiosity. This would be the opportunity to get acquainted with living spaces other than their own homes and to hear the anecdotes of what is contained in the homes of others in their neighborhood. They would often take to the sheep and cow sheds, poultry and pet pens, pigeon towers, parrot and bird cages, and the like. At other times, they would be dazzled by the antics of collectibles, tools, and equipment related to the work of the owner of the house. In the house of Al-Serafy, there was a room full of wall clocks, and in other houses, there were collections of carpets; and in yet another house, there was a bride's room whose walls and ceilings were decorated with mirrors and gleaming frills. In Zuleikh's house, there are rooms and corridors full of rusty swords, colored flags, and the remains of what was used in religious processions of Ashura, in memory of Imam Husain, and on other popular holidays.

The women of the house and their visitors from among the neighbors would usually gather in the courtyard of our house to wash rice and help each other in preparing food, roasting and pounding coffee, or kneading flour, preparing henna, or doing needlework. They would do this voluntarily to pay respect to my mother, who used to preach to them daily and on religious occasions.

They would occupy their time until the noon call to prayer with news and amusing tales, or quarreling over controversy in any matter. And perhaps the voices would be raised after that, and the tongues would lengthen, and the movements of the heads, arms, and eyes would proceed with great nervousness until the weakest of them would surrender; thus, tears would flow and sorrows would be washed away, so that the course of the meeting would resume as it began, or in some cases it would be shut down to be resumed the next day.

The boys would take advantage of the women's preoccupation to satisfy their curiosity, but when the people of the house became aware of their presence, at the sound of a baby provoked by movement from his sleep, or the roof shaking under their footsteps and some dust falling, or the entry of the man who supplies drinking water with his barking donkey, or the like, their fate would be immediate expulsion from the house, coupled with humiliation. And the last of them usually did not survive, while they were on their escape journey, from a blow to the head or shoulder by a broom made of palm fronds. Homes that would not allow children in would not usually mind providing thirsty children with water, which was a legitimate request and a common tradition. The dispute was often resolved over the recovery of the lost ball when it returned from the house, either intact or having been stabbed with a knife. In the latter case, the owner of the ball would mourn his misfortune.

As a way of expressing his indignation, he would often pelt the house's front door with stones, while the rest of the group would move on to another game, such as "gob glean," which was played with a wooden racket and a small piece of wood that the opponent must grab before it falls to the ground, a primitive baseball of sorts; otherwise, it would be considered a foul. And every foul would earn a throw from the racket holder toward a further distance. Often, these fouls would accumulate until the players reached the woods outside of city limits, at the confluence of the orchards. The loser would be required to start running back to the playing position from where the penalty space ended, and he must shout loudly. If he stops shouting early, he will earn another penalty kick.

However, the sight of the land near the cemetery and the orchards surrounding it would often tempt the boys to turn away from their games and instead engage in hunting birds. Before beginning that task, they must try extracting an earthworm to be used as bait in traps. They would catch the earthworm by inserting a dry, sharp palm leaf into the holes of the earth and extracting it quickly and skillfully, and they would eventually find a worm sticking to it.

The boys would occupy themselves with other events of the day as well, such as wedding ceremonies, funerals, births, and homes where banquets were held, where food utensils and trays were carried by old ladies from one house to another. Large mirrors and sweet dishes would also be carried on the heads of women to wedding parties held by neighbors, to be returned back after the wedding ceremony. This was in addition to the public holidays of the National Day Celebration, Ramadan (the month of fasting), Eids (religious festivals), Mawlids (Profit Mohamed's birthday, peace be upon him), and others. Young boys did not need to be invited, for they were always present wherever there was an event taking place. Their age and the family name of their parents would allow them the freedom to roam as they pleased among the community of men and women alike, but even these joys did not equal the joy of going to the market at night. The children would await the Night of Adornment to celebrate the seating of His Highness the Sheikh, King of Bahrain, with great anticipation, as the markets would be decorated with colors, lights, flags, and ornamental leaves. The roads were covered with carpets, sherbet, and coffee, and sweets were served. Rose water was sprinkled, the air was perfumed with the smoke of incense, and shopkeepers would visit each other and stay up until the late part of the night in overwhelming joy.

I would always become enamored with this unique scene—the markets in which life would stop and people would dissipate as soon as sunset arrived. Then after that, they would return to the Night of Adornment with all their momentum and joys, except that there was no selling or buying among them. Even the lunatic *tanbura* player (which is a primitive playing instrument), with his slender brown and long body, would not forget to return to the market, as he did every day, immersed in a semi-coma, humming repeatedly in his soft, faint voice, "Salem beat Salloma... Salem says!"

= 3 =
The Nail and the Revolving Toy

*

I used to go to the market to collect my daily allowance money from my father (at that time worth in between half an Indian rupee to one) to buy sweets, or to buy toys for playing, such as a small tennis ball, a whirligig and nail, glass marbles for playing the staple game, and so on. I used to also go to the tailor shop for new clothes, with the permission of my father, to have two new Arabian garments made throughout the year. The whirligig was sold by Al-Bohra Indian merchants, including the string without a nail. This toy seemed to be very anciently ingrained in our history. In the Pre-Islamic Era, the poet Imru' Al-Qays called it "Khudhruf Al-Walid" in his famous *mu-allaqa* poetry, which was written with gold letters and was hung around the walls of the Holy Kaa'ba in Mecca.

Fixing the nail to a whirligig at the blacksmith shop was an experience full of excitement and curiosity. And the road to the blacksmith market was located at the onset of the popular traditional coffee shops, full of people of varying ethnicities, most of them seamen or workers who came to enjoy the voices of the popular local singers while grabbing something to eat or drink. Small boys were forbidden by their parents, because of religious beliefs, to sit in such places or to sing or listen to songs from phonographs. And although I knew that it was forbidden for me to hang around them, I was seldom able to resist the temptation to stop next to the phonograph and contemplate it carefully whenever I passed by it. What I admired most-on the phonograph was a funny picture of a dog listening to his (master's voice.)

The market paths branched off at the head of my daily path, and their names varied according to the type of profession or trade. The entrance to the market for fabrics and clothing (linen or cloth) started from the cotton combing shop, where the cotton of old beds and pillows were nicely combed, upholstered, and cleaned so that they could be used once again. I used to help my father to carry old beds and pillows there. I always felt a sense of astonishment at the sight of the big cotton combing machine, which captivated my curiosity, while a man would be playing the white cotton song on it. The cotton would fly through the air and then descend onto the face of the player, as well as his eyebrows, eyelashes, and mustache, resembling white snow.

I used to walk to the Bohra market, which was the wide courtyard located in the heart of the market, and it was more like a festival and a permanent and mobile exhibition at the same time for all the goods and services that were not found in the other markets. In this courtyard, old mattresses were laid on the ground as a seat for veiled women in black, selling needles, threads, scissors, buttons, and so on, as well as street vendors selling cakes, bread, sweets, and drinks; bakeries of every kind; sellers in auctions—places where bettors would throw coins on flat dishes—and popular restaurants smelling of smoky fumes and the aroma of freshly cooked food. It was always accompanied by a large crowd of beggars and loafers.

Barbers and cuppers occupied the front entrance. I deliberately used to pass between the rows of the cupping clients with their heads lowered to the ground so they would not see the cupper. I was trying in vain to know the secret of those bloody cups and the meaning of the red circles and bulges they left on the backs and heads of those who surrendered to the old cupper, who would be squatted down, moving in this posture among his customers to change the cups—slowly—as if he was amusing himself by torturing a group of sinners.

*

I used to buy a whirligig and head to the blacksmith market, passing the Al-Safarin market, i.e., the coppersmith market, stopping to watch the process of the whitening of copper pots, in which more than one person participated. The master took care of the hammering of pots, on whose walls there were shiny crystals that resembled tattoos, and made them revolve with his hands and legs. The others, who were often the sons of the master of craftsmanship, would perform the cleaning process, standing on their feet inside the concave copper pot after placing the cleaning stones in its hollow, and then they would perform dance-like movements of twisting. The process of whistling and bleaching, the materials that flew into the fire through clouds of smoke, and the suffocating odors that accompanied the whole process did not tempt me to stay any longer than that, and it was only a matter of minutes until I reached the blacksmith market. I squat beside Black Smother, with his hand on the whirligig, narrowly avoiding the sparks of fire that were flying toward him from the other side. He took the whirligig and examined it first, to appraise its quality.

This did not prevent him from placing it next to him as a sign of acceptance and waiting for my turn. When the moment of truth had come and the nail was set in the burning flame, the blacksmith took hold of the whirligig with his left hand, which was streaked with ashes, and grabbed the nail and fixed it in place.

Sometimes the whirligig might split into two halves if the nail was too big. I became unable to contain the tears that streamed down my face. The blacksmith—repeating a sentence that must have been routine to him: Go back to your father and buy a new one with an appropriately sized nail, and I will fix the nail free of charge.

During periods of waiting and anticipation, I would look around and listen to what was being said in the adult community. But my memory did not have the capacity to memorize everything I heard or recollected, but I remember There was once a seller at the entrance to the market, complaining about his life and misfortune to those around him, repeating, "My misfortune is like when I hung my clothes out to dry…" So, his neighbor volunteered to complete the verse, "On a hot summer July day, it will start to rain."

I also heard the story of the father who came to the blacksmith to complain of a quarrel between their two sons, so the blacksmith said to the complainer, "If your son hit our son, he must be disciplined. And if our son hits your son…" Then he turned to his son and said to him, "Light up the fire," meaning that it didn't matter.

I also remembered well what the blacksmith once said to the person sitting next to him, "He who sits near the fire must accept the sparks." Finally, finally I jumped with joy after getting the whirligig's nail fixed, blissfully ignoring some holes burned by the sparks into my clothes. Then I went to the sweet water supplier, originating from the Alhunainia sweet water spring.

I used to search for the water supplier, then convey to him the number of sweet water skins required for the house, according to what my father had dictated to me. I often swallowed a sip of fresh water from the mouth of the skin pipe and poured some of it on my chest and shoulders in order to cool myself. Then I got up on his donkey, and the water supplier, along with the water load, followed behind us. If I came across some boys with whom I used to play, I ignored them proudly, turning my back to them while riding on the donkey. Not far from me, I could hear the baker's clicks with the dough-pivot on the table and smell the aroma of freshly baked bread calling for me, so I would ignore it, citing what I would find back at home, but I could not resist letting my thoughts wander and remembering my usual spot that I would stand in at the bakery shop in front of that huge, wide table that allowed, despite its shortness, a small pair of feet to extend from underneath it, while I was intent on cutting the good parts off of the spoiled bread and chewing it very carefully without making a sound, keeping it unknown to the owner. The baker was engaged in a frantic race between the speed of turning the dough without disturbing the rule of clicks on the table and performing the maneuver to get it into the oven. Sitting next to him at ground level, opening its brutal mouth as if it were one of those seated, except that this overly cozy way of sitting was unbearable. However, he accepted it reluctantly and endured the glow of the fire blazing in his face, along with his damaged fingers, the rottenness of the bread, the overcrowding of customers, and the many debts left unpaid. Despite all of that, it did not prevent him from greeting any and all customers in a respectful manner.

When we reached the house, the water supplier entered the tall house gate, which was stuffed with huge nails. I would never wait to open the big door but instead slip into the small gap (the gap of the door made for single entry) and surprise the family of the house with whatever my current news may be, causing confusion among them at times. Then the people of the house prepared for the passage of the stranger, who walked over to the place where he would pour the water into the big earthenware pot, which was called a *jahla*. He would make plenty of noise to notify the ladies of the house of his presence in order for them to cover themselves properly. Then he would amble slowly toward the exit door until he heard someone calling for him to wait; thus, he would sit on the mat on the bench, usually facing the guest room, and be offered refreshments while separated from the house by a thick curtain of burlap or heavy cloth. I would surprise myself by how much time I would spend awaiting the head of the family's arrival home, and I would be overwhelmed by my feelings of boredom. There were no toys in the house either. The majority of parents at that time did not care to buy toys for their children; thus, the youngsters would be forced to invent means of entertainment for themselves. Whenever I got hungry, I would stealthily throw a few potatoes in the fire under one of the pots. I recalled my intense longing for roasted potatoes on a particular day when I, along with the other boys, rushed to the place of the great fire pit in the vegetable market and saw a huge quantity of potatoes that had been tarnished by the fire that no one dared to approach. While I was roasting my potatoes, a water supplier arrived with his cart to deliver discounted drinking water from springs and wells to be used for the family of the house as well as their visitors and also for cooking. The sweet, expensive water from Alhunainia was only to be used by my parents. I become aware of the near arrival of the water supplier and his cart, and so do the people of the house, because of the braying of his donkey that is dragging the cart, along with the creaking of its two big wheels. The cart was carrying a huge wooden barrel tied with iron collars. Then the water supplier flung the door wide open to deliver water from the water skin. He was famous for his activity and strength, carrying one water skin on his shoulder and the other under his armpit, then he finished pouring the water quickly and stopped in front of the door before exiting, not to wait for food or drink but to draw two lines on the wall at the entrance with the black grease of the wheels by which he would adjust the calculation of the monthly consumption; then he left.

Then I went back to loitering inside the house. I watched out the door to satisfy my curiosity until I saw the grocer, who sold the farmer's produce for cash or bartered for a handful of bread, rice, flour, dates, or other types of food products. I also waited for the Persian man who collected old clothes to embroider with Alzary, i.e., an old type of gold-plated thread, and a Jewish cloth vender who always lugged around a big bag on top of his shoulders, along with the man who sold Manchoose, which is a small type of fish.

Mr. Charles Belgraive, the English adviser to the government of Bahrain, made fire alarming bell in different places in the city of Manama, and passersby will ring the bell continually when fire takes place. People will be rushing for help. As if their minds were blown, I used to join them, with a safe distance from the fire, before the Municipality Fire Team arrived.

Back to my house, I would harass and tamper with everything I touched. At times, I would pretend that I was washing at the well, as most households used to dig water wells in their houses to be used for bathing and cleaning utensils and dishes, while I was actually entertaining myself with buckets and pouring water in vain. Some china plates or pottery utensils might have fallen out of my hand and broken. So, my mother would threaten me with punishment. (Note: In addition to the three sources to get water as mentioned above, before municipality water became available in 1942, some houses preferred to drink from water called *shuraiba*. This water was collected from sweet water at the bottom of the sea from springs flowing from high mountains in the Arabian Peninsula.)

And I would continue to play with anything I could reach until I felt that a state of readiness had spread throughout the house and I heard the words, "O God," repeated over and over again—then I would be certain that my father has just returned, so I would run to hug him at the door and escort him inside, clinging to his clothes until he settled down, then we would leave each other alone. But as soon as my father was free to pray, I would sneak back to my father—adding to the surprise—and when I would find my father immersed in prayer or in supplication, his eyes overflowing with tears from fear of God, and bending to the ground, I did not deviate from his determination to climb onto his back. The father, after prayer, would hold me to his chest and listen to me with words of love and tenderness that reassured my heart and quenched my thirst for love, making my eyes shine in an abundance of joy and confidence. I would feel then that I was at home with those I loved and those who loved him, and I would taste the sweetness of returning home in the end and the euphoria of belonging after feeling lost between the neighborhood paths, the market paths, and the intrusive journey into the adult community.

Reward and Punishment

Nonetheless, a young boy in general would soon learn, while he is in the climax of his ecstasy in love, an important life lesson: that joy does not last and that home life—just like the reality of everything in life—has two faces.

The boy's housewife mother was obliged to report the occurrences of the day, including everything that took place in it to his father. If she did that as soon as the master of the house arrived—because of her tenseness on that day—the verse would be reversed, as he would have realized that the patience of the housewife with the transgressions of the young ones had reached its limit, and if the disciplinarian stick was still in its spot and close enough within reach, his father would grab the transgressor and start beating him, while the other sons fled to the roof of the house and, if the pursuit extended further, on to the roofs of the neighbors' houses.

The angry father, while inflicting his punishment, would not neglect to recite the list of violations while holding the boy down, then would count them one by one with each stroke of the stick as if he were reading an account statement. The boy would exaggerate in screaming and asking for help, repeating, "I repent! I repent! By almighty God!" Until his voice became hoarse, or the father's fingers withered, or the mother interfered, or the neighbors would sometimes even intervene if the punishment exceeded its limits.

Children were usually disciplined because of quarrels, disobedience, neglecting their duties, neglecting their prayers, disturbing the neighbors, as well as avoiding their noon naps (siestas), and abandoning the shade of the house during the blistering summer days.

The manifestations of activity in the house and the neighborhood in general stopped at nap time, so the noise subsided. The movement stopped, the washing of pots stopped at the well, and the curtains would come down as the roosters and chickens were banished to a distant place. The wall clock alone worked without objection, and if the pendulum swaying to the right and left made a monotonous sound that brought sleep to the eyes, its chimes defied—without a doubt—the decision to remain silent, as if it were proving that time must announce its existence and move on.

In the evening, the father would return loaded with sweets, or nuts, bread, date cookies, or any other so-called "*hajour*" in order to initiate the reconciliation ceremonies, which were for the boy to kiss his father's hand and ask for forgiveness, declaring repentance, and for the father to embrace him with kindness and contentment, to dine together, and then to sleep.

Most houses at that time had no electricity, so the families would sleep on the roof under the open sky in the summer months and awaken in the morning with dampened beds and clothes due to the mist that fell during the summer nights.

Listening to Parents' Conversations

One summer's night, while lying on my bed on the roof of the house, pretending to be asleep, I overheard a conversation between my mother and father. The mother conveyed to the father the latest news regarding neighborhood happenings, arranging the eldest son's and daughter's marriage, also about visitors of the house, and requirements of the house, etc. The father in turn conveyed his opinion on the housekeeping plan for tomorrow and the day after, the maintenance projects, his next travel plan, and the reception of incoming guests. As for news of trade and business, it was limited to important news only because trade plans were to remain a secret, as was the custom of merchants. Among that important news was the big fire in the vegetable market. I heard the exciting details of this fire, which had spread beyond the vegetable market to its surroundings, but it had not reached, thank God, the father's shop. The father also expressed his happiness that he ordered his fellow sailors from the country of Oman to remove the safe deposit of money and important files to a secure location. Then he dwelled on praising the chivalry and magnanimity they showed and how they came to the rescue when they heard the news. Thus, I recalled the Omani sailors' kindness when they used to take me with them to the sea in their big boats that they called "*sanbuks*," and how I used to spend my day enjoying the life of the sea and the traditions of the Omanis, which differed somewhat from the usual along these coasts. I would be greatly amused by going back and forth with them in a large group in small long boats and rowing together, as if they were large, symmetrical fins of large fish, and every sailor behind an oar participated with the group in singing with one unified voice and a monotonous tone and a rhythm that increased faster with the increase in enthusiasm for rowing while chanting, "In my hand I carry the best sword," or in other words, it indicated courage and strength of determination.

And the drowsiness that crept in with the breeze saturated with dew drops overcame my little eyelids, and they fell asleep on the image of the sea and visions of waves and the flapping of sails and oars. So, I missed out on hearing further news from my parents that interested me so much.

Whoever Teaches Me a Letter

As for the important news, which I had missed that night, it was about taking me to a teacher of the Holy

Book (the Qur'an). When the time came, the Father ordered one morning that I wear the clothes that had been bought for the occasion, and I did, then to put on a waistcoat of silk brocade and put on a ring and put on my favorite pair of sandals, and when my father put in my right hand a bound book, I knew that it was *Juz Amma* (the last of thirty sections) of the Noble Qur'an and that he was on his way to the teacher of the Qur'an, also referred to as the '*Mutawa.*'

The Father held my hand to walk with him to the teacher. It was my custom when I followed my father's footsteps to wait until the Father's grip was relaxed while walking, so I would drop his hand lightly to lag behind him slightly in walking and take in the exciting sights of the road. There were theaters for runaway cats and poultry, seating for beggars, and suitable-for-acting as adults who picked up leftover bread from the middle of the road and squished it into the holes in the wall and into its cracks—where ant houses abound—in observance of the sanctity of God's grace, but the Father's grip on this day remained tight. The boy found it necessary to ignore all of this spectacle and follow rigidly along with his father's strenuous steps. Even he forgot—because he was so preoccupied with what his father had planned for him this morning—to perform his familiar, loving habit of stopping at the wall of the neighbor's house opposite their house, in order to dig into the base, of the wall, where he used to discover his usual treasure, which was eight annas or sometimes one Indian rupee, which that kind and admirable neighbor, Al-Sayyid Husayn Alhadramy, used to tuck into the dirt under the window site as a courtesy to the boy whenever he went out in the morning to go to work, as if this virtuous man, out of his excessive politeness and humanity, was embarrassed to appear as a giver to this boy whom he loves as one of his sons, out of appreciation for him and out of respect for his father's friendship. He gave this little boy the feeling of joy by extracting his treasure with his hand after pointing to him from afar to the specific location without speaking!

The father tightened his grip on the boy's hand whenever it slacked a little, and he reminded him of the dangers of slowing down his walk, citing the last time when the boy slowed down and left his father's grip and a snake slithered through a hole in an old wall and fell on his head. The snake was about to wrap around his neck or bite him, and he would have been even more terrified had it not been for his father to save him.

The teacher greeted the father with the respect and welcome that befitted him, then turned to the boy with a gleaming smile on his face, waiting for the father to start talking so that he could figure out how to deal with the newcomer.

He did not wait for long, and then the father surprised him by instructing him to treat his son well. The father recited some verses of the Qur'an and phrases, such as the old saying of Imam Ali: "Discipline him for seven (years), teach him for seven, and educate him for seven. Then let him go as he pleases." The teacher did not hear what he had expected to hear, like what other fathers would say, "I gave you my son as meat, so you give him back as bones," i.e., because of the frequent beatings and discipline. For this and in response to the directions, the teacher put aside his long stick that shone from wiping it so frequently with oil in order to preserve its freshness, and he came up to the boy with a bright smile. Then his father gave him two eggs to break under his feet in honor or possibly to ward off evil spirits. Then my father recited Surat al-Fatihah from the Holy Qur'an.

As soon as the father left, the teacher brought the boy with him to the classroom, and the yelling of the boys in the absence of the teacher had resounded in the sky. But their sudden silence upon his arrival did not satisfy him, so the punishment was quickly inflicted upon them without discrimination, while the boy settled in the new seat, which was made of wicker, awaiting his unknown fate.

The boy missed that smile on the face of the teacher after entering the group of boys, except when the teacher came to collect his monthly fees at his father's office or during what the teacher called the "egg sharing," i.e., each boy brought six eggs from his house and delivered them to the teacher for dyeing the eggs with colors, and the teacher handed over to the boys only three colored eggs after dyeing, keeping three eggs for himself—a clever way to increase the teacher's income. The boys could encounter a smile on the face of the teacher also when celebrating the occasion of any of the boys who completed their memorization of the Qur'an, as he was expecting a gift from their fathers.

With the exception of those few occasions, the relationship between the teacher and the boys proceeded according to that famous saying that was repeated on every occasion, "Whoever teaches me a letter, I become his slave."

= 4 =
My School Memories

The Portuguese Castle

The Portuguese Castle (*qalat al Portugal*) was my favorite place for a weekend break or sometimes to escape from school. Whenever I reminisce on my childhood days, I find that the Bahrain Fort—as we used to call it—still holds a prominent place in those memories. Above its high towers, I felt as though I was looking out over the whole world. Through the carefully cut holes in its walls (mainly used for hiding guns), I seemed to have an extraordinary ability to eavesdrop and watch those who were approaching and to harm any of them if I wished. I chose my path up and down the castle very carefully, as I had no doubt at the time that the castle was inhabited by evil spirits. Moreover, it was a scene for many thieves and criminals. And whenever I stumbled upon one of its stones and it trembled under my feet, I thought the stone yawned as if it had just woken up from a long slumber.

I often stared at the rocks with round and crumpled hollows in gloomy silence, remembering the old saying that they contained a treasure chest that thieves had opened, and those hollows seemed to me like mouths that were about to cry out toward the thieves and perpetrators for what they had done in stealing the treasures of the ancestors who had deposited them in the rocks.

Thus, as I hastened to go down, avoiding as much as possible the untracked paths of the deep pit around the castle for fear of serpents and scorpions, I took rest under the shade of one of the great eroded towers, where time seemed to me like an insatiable ogre, ravaging from those towers day by day. As for the secret of this castle, which received the arrivals with a grim face from which flew gunpowder and sparks and then did not dare to turn its face to people, earth, and life around it except through thick walls of fear and apprehension.

The return trip from the castle also had a mood and a taste. I knew the directions from the road through gardens with orchards and villages, and then I would pass by the fruit trees overlooking the street. From the site of the lemon trees, from the beginning, to the other areas full of pomegranates, then all the way to the *Knar* trees, where the sight of the fruits hanging on the sides of the road and the thought of picking some of them would sometimes obscure the imagination of the castle, these mixed feelings would vanish in me, to be replaced by an unparalleled sense of pride. The castle was the farthest point that a little boy could reach because he had no means of transportation except for a bicycle that often broke down in the middle of the road. Then fear would seep into my soul, and I would become alarmed.

More often than not, the help would arrive at the hands of Abu Dawood. And this Abu Dawood—as we used to call him—is the storyteller to the customers of his small shop, along with being the pioneer of risks, the champion of athletics, the engineer of wheels, and the conjurer of *jinn* and spirits. He had learned the profession of goldsmithing from his father, and he used to visit the castle every time he found a way to do so, as if he had an inheritance there, fearing he might lose it. And this Abu Dawood became recognized by most of the people who walked by, and the farmers turned toward him, and the boys pointed at him whenever he passed by. One time, Abu Dawood let me in on a serious, secret matter. He said that he had found the treasure he was looking for in the castle, and he needed someone to conceal the news and carry this treasure with him. He loaded me behind his bicycle with a straw container (*jafeer*) that contained a large piece of red glowing stone and small pieces of it that fell from time to time on one of my feet and caused it to bleed and itch. He thought himself a goldsmith and that he could extract gold from the stone. The result of the examination was a shattering of dreams. And here was Abu Dawood, using his experience in craftsmanship to finally distinguish between dust and gold.

Public and Private Education

After memorizing the entirety of the Noble Qur'an, my older brother accompanied me to Al-Ahlia private school, which was the school run by Mr. Abdul Rassol Altajir. The whole atmosphere was very different from what I was familiar with while studying with the Qur'an teacher. For the first time, I entered into a large classroom filled with students of varying ages and educational and social levels. Following this long row, there was a second room in the corner, in which the graduate students were trained to use typewriter would sit.

The schoolmaster, Mr. Altajir, sat at a separate table that overlooked both sides, and he was the only teacher in charge of that impressive number of students! The students took a seat in front of his table. The classroom walls were equipped with glass cabinets with shelves, upon which there was an abundance of bound books, neatly arranged and classified, which was a strange and impelling sight and a sudden shift for me from what was familiar to me of the simplicity and primitiveness of the Qur'an teacher's property. Also, the students were granted the freedom of entry and exit as they pleased, as if the school doors were always open. Students did not study in groups or classes; rather, those who wanted to take the lesson would go directly to the teacher's table and wait for their turn. Headmaster Altajir would accept the task of teaching any number of students, regardless of how many, all of them sitting in front of him individually, awaiting his turn, and would start with one of them and listen to him read out the lesson while he was busy correcting the notebooks or writing a new lesson plan for another student. Yet this did not prevent him from paying attention to correcting the student's mistakes in reading from time to time.

Then the teacher would alternate between this cluster of students, taking advantage of the time overlap, with the skill of a master chess player against a group of opponents.

This educational method of the Ahlia private school, which was similar to fast food restaurants, was a suitable way, in the early 1930s, for Bahrainis to learn English, basic mathematics, and typing in order to become able to apply for jobs at the BAPCO oil company, as well as other local and foreign establishments in Bahrain, in addition to government jobs offered by Bahrain's Governmental Secretary, Mr. W. Belgrave.

A large crowd had graduated from this school, and there was not a doubt that most of them—if not all of them—made special mention of this dedicated professor who was committed to his work, his virtue in spreading education, and sacrificing his time, health, and comfort, and was his utmost happiest to do so. As for the wages for teaching in those days, it was two Indian rupees per month, and it was not paid regularly!

I discovered in myself an overwhelming desire to learn more quickly, so I was not satisfied with only one lesson per day, and I would come early to take that one lesson. Then I would prepare the required duties, and when I found an empty seat, I would take another lesson. Sometimes I used to take three or four lessons in a day.

Mr. Altajir was kind enough to allow me to take more than one lesson a day, contrary to other students who used to take one lesson a day only. He used to show me that he was aware of my abilities. After any additional lesson, he used to remove his reading glasses and stare intensely into my eyes. I imagined that what he meant by that glare was that he wanted me to tell my father that two rupees per month for lessons was not enough.

In addition to the lessons of Arabic, English, and arithmetic, I used to greatly enjoy the calligraphy lessons. I would look forward to what he would write at the top of the page in red and in the beautiful calligraphic font of the verses that were renewed with each lesson—for example, "It is morals that grow like plants if they are watered with blessings of good doing."

I also preserved this satirical verse from him about religious hypocrites: "He walks with a turban like a tower on top of him, but upon a hill of hypocrisy." These poems awakened my first inclination to read and taste poetry.

I discovered my desire to transfer from Altajir's school to Bahrain government school in Manama, namely: Alkhalifa primary school for boys—as it was called at the time—seeking acceptance of my father, may God have mercy on him. In addition to the school being close to our house, my father had fond memories of this school. He was among its first founders in 1927, when its name was the Al-Jaafari private school for children. My father also helped in contracting with its first director, Muhammad Saeed bin Juma'a, and a number of its Iraqi professors. He took over its fund until it was transferred after a few years to the governmental administration, and since then he frequently told us the story of his liquidation of the school's debts and then of his visit to the governmental advisor, Mr. Belgrave, and handing him the remaining amount of the school's account balance, which had deepened the advisor's astonishment and admiration. Then the name of the school had been changed during the forties to "Al Gharbia" and then to "Abu Bakr Al Siddik."

It was said that the school director and his fellow Iraqi teachers were imbued with the spirit of "*Futuwwa,*" and wanted to form in the school a scout troupe similar to the one formed in the time of King Ghazi of Iraq, reflecting the national enthusiasm that prevailed in Iraq at the time, so they established a scout troupe and equipped them with musical instruments, and they went around the neighborhoods and markets in Manama city, chanting some national anthems, such as: "O Children of Bahrain, rise to the top and raise your heads among nations of the world," and the like.

None of that was happening when I started at the school, but I remember there was a closed room. We were eager to see what was inside. We heard commotion in the inner school yard, and when we exited the classroom, we saw a group of police officers evacuating multitudes of brass musical instruments. Some of the instruments were rusty, so they were cleaned, any traces of spears or sticks or anything else that belonged to the scouts being fully eliminated; thus, the features of the past almost completely disappeared, even if there was only one trace of them left—the *Futuwwa* shield, which was hung on the wall in a prominent spot in the courtyard and upon which was written, "*Wa a iddo*," i.e., "Be ready for them"—a part of a Qur'anic verse meaning, "Be prepared," which had become the slogan of *Futuwwa*. The students alternated in standing in front of this shield, examining it, each of them taking his turn to utter this phrase and try to extract its meaning.

About six months had passed at Altajir's school, and when the time came for me to attend the Al-Khalifa school, I met in the administration's office one of the assistants who was about to admit me to the first grade had the director not suddenly entered—the headmaster

Salem Al-Arayed, may God have mercy on him—and he tested my knowledge and admitted me to the fourth grade instead. I was seven years old. Unfortunately for me, I entered during the Arabic dictation class. More than two months had passed since the opening of the school year. The format of the dictation notebook by writing the name, date, and class was not familiar in my previous studies, which irked my Arabic teacher, Mr. Al-Mihza, so he wrote at the top of the page in red ink, "29 Sha'ban in the year 1357 A.H." followed with a strong slap to my own face, so that he would have what it seemed he had wanted. I can still feel the sting of that slap to this day.

I was not able to handle the sudden change in the education system and lesson format, so I yielded a disappointing result. I received my report card—it was so small that it resembled a passport—containing my quarterly results. Written on the last page was the total grade for the whole school year—55%! The headcount of students in my class had exceeded 64. Under it, the principal, Salem Al-Arayeed, had written in red font the phrase: "Strive, so you may not regret."

In the following year, however, when I entered fifth grade, I achieved great success and achieved the rank of first in my class. Having listened to the wise advice of my headmaster, I did not allow myself the chance to fall into a state of regret; thus, I maintained this rank throughout my primary and secondary school years.

Since I was the youngest student in every class I entered, this paradox became the subject of frequent discussion. The lessons in the primary school were limited to Arabic with its branches, English, arithmetic, history, geography, sports, and religion. Schools at that time did not recognize the need for kindergarten, art education, music, handicrafts, or means of illustration. Because of the conditions of the Second World War, textbooks were scarce, as were pamphlets. I studied at the hands of Palestinian teachers, including Aref Mahmoud, Amr Shehda, Youssef Al-Dajani, and Nadim Al-Hallaq. As for the rest of the teachers, among them were the teachers Ahmad Al-Muhaza, Khalil Zubari, Ahmad Jassem, Abd Ali Abbas, Shawl—who was Jewish—and Ali Al-Madani, and then there was the principal, Salem Al-Arayedh, who used to teach us the arithmetic section from a huge book that was completely in the English language! During the lesson on religion, Jews and non-Muslims were allowed to leave the classroom, and the Muslim students were divided between two lessons, each with a private teacher. The non-Muslim students were overjoyed to play sports in the courtyard or to buy some food from nearby shops.

One of the things I remember distinctly is that the English Director of Education, Mr. Wallace from the British Council in Bahrain, was a reckless person who did not care to observe local traditions, and that he surprised the school one day before noon with a group of doctors and summoned all the students of the school for a medical examination without making any exceptions. Most of the students were embarrassed by being examined in the nude in front of all of the others and raised amongst themselves riots of grumbles, upon which the director treated them harshly. When the time for their return home had turned late, many parents called the school in protest, and most of them were not convinced of the justifications given by the administration for this reckless behavior.

As for the secretary of government, Mr. Belgrave, he ordered the students (during World War II) to dig trenches around schoolyards and trained students and teachers to use them as shelters during illusory raids accompanied by sirens. Everyone used to go down to these dirt trenches whenever raids took place, until they ended!

One day, His Highness, the late Amir Sheikh Hamad bin Isa Al-Khalifa, visited our school, and I was in the sixth grade. Our teacher—knowing that His Highness was fond of geography—chose me to go up to the blackboard to explain the subject, specifically how to travel from Bahrain to famous Indian cities by ship. Thus, I chose to draw a map of the Gulf and India and then "travel" from Bahrain, passing through the most important cities in the Indian subcontinent, detailing for what each of them was famous for. I was very pleased with the praise I received from His Highness the Emir and the administration. Ironically, later, when I grew up, I had the wonderful opportunity of visiting a lot of the world's most famous cities, except for those particular Indian cities!

The years of World War II at this stage reminded me of the overwhelming war propaganda materials that were distributed in the classrooms, along with some newspapers, and I remembered the rapidly circulating magazine "The Arab Listener," issued by BBC radio in London. Also bound small paper toys, we used to turn them quickly to see Mr. Churchill rising to the top and Nazi Hitler falling down.

Cinema films of the war were shown in schools, in cities, and in villages alike.

I remember also the manifestations of terror among the women and children when "Sikh" soldiers from India crossed the alleys of Manama at a sprint, the doors were closed, and the neighborhood would collectively stop breathing until the last of them disappeared from sight. In the end, no one would be able to forget the days where there was a great shortage of food and necessities.

At that time, I was fond of reading incessantly. In the fourth and fifth grades, I read *Jawahar al-Adab, Kalila wa Dimna by Ibn Almuqaffa, and One Thousand and One Nights*, and in the fifth and sixth grades, I balanced my reading between the books of the famous Zaki Mubarak, the novels of Al-Manfaluti, the works of Salama Musa and Al-Mazini, all from Egypt, the poetry of the Diaspora by Arab writers in America, and finally Plato's Republic!

= 5 =
All Roads Lead to Secondary School

Its name, when I enrolled in 1941, was Al-Khalifia Secondary School. It was still brand new. That is because, while I was in sixth grade, the Director of Education in Bahrain was Mr. Wakelin from the British Council in Bahrain. He came in one day to select a group of students in our class. I was not among them because of my young age, but my brother Hussein was among them. And it was assumed that the same phenomenon happened in all other government schools. Then these selected students were combined and admitted in the form of two classrooms, to be called the "college" with all the glamor, gloss, and great distinction that this name bore. A site was chosen for the college, "the headquarters of the old Eastern Bank," the Al-Qusaibi building near the market.

Then the college was closed after its first and last year. I was in the seventh grade of my school. Mr.

Wakelin removed the students from the "college" site to another big house under the name of Bahrain Secondary School. He also arranged for successful students in my class to join other students at the secondary school. I was one of them after getting the highest grades on the final exams. Some of the students dispersed, and some of them enrolled at the Industrial School, which was new. The beginning of the forties was a stage of labor and birth in the history of education in Bahrain, witnessing the diligent Director of Education, Mr. Wakelin, with his activity and vitality under the auspices of His Highness the Emir of the country and the guidance of the Minister of Education, the late Sheikh Abdullah bin Isa Al Khalifa.

The choice of place for the "college" fell on a large house owned by the notable merchant Mansour Al-Arayedh on Sheikh Abdullah Street in Manama to become the headquarters of the secondary school. Next to the house was a small complex of the same owner, which included a workshop for goldsmithing and pearl trade as well as a meeting place for pearl merchants. Soon, this aspect was transformed into an internal hostel for students outside the capital of Manama. Subsequently, the offices of the Director of Education and the Public Library were later moved to the same area.

The secondary school consisted of three classrooms, one of which overlooked the zoo (Al-Baghsha) with its charming view, and the other two were on Sheikh Abdullah Street. And located in the middle were the principal's office and the teachers' lounge, each of which had the important advantage of having electric ceiling fans!

Most of the businessmen and merchants—except for a few of them—walked to the market from their nearby homes, in many cases meaning that they would pass by the secondary school on their way. Some of them liked to visit the secondary school on their way to the market, whether to check on their children, simply to see the features of this new educational edifice, or even to donate some money. The reception ceremony took place as follows: the bell would ring, and the students would be summoned to the schoolyard to organize themselves in long lines. Then the principal would take a stroll with the visiting guests, showing off the students in what looked like a guard inspection ceremony. A chant like, "Peace be upon you from me, O land of my ancestors," would commence. Another staff member would come and recite a piece of poetry, then the director would whistle, and a number of students would rush to form a human pyramid, on top of which a student climbed and recited a line of Arabic poetry. Then the guest would speak as he liked, and he might pass through some rows, denote some money, or leave, bidding farewell at the door. As for the vocalist, he was always one of two people: Abd al-Rahman al-Shirawi or Hassan al-Madani, both of whom were distinguished by the beauty of their voices. As for the reciter of poetry, it was often Sheikh Khalid bin Muhammad Al Khalifa. He would be grasping a large *sibha* (similar to a rosary but used by Muslims) between his fingers and swaying back and forth while reciting verses of poetry composed by the poet Ali Al-Jarim, immersed in performing them with a somber recitation. The poetry reflected the horrors of World War I:

"I wonder who stole the sleepiness from my eyes and left me to suffer in pain, and who caused singing birds not to sing in joy.

And who threw thorns into my bed and left me with fear and unrest."

... continuing to the end of the poem.

It seems that the poet composed the verses in the aftermath of the First World War, but they still expressed, with the same essence, the tragedies of the Second World War, which was raging at the time. As for the one who climbed to the top of the pyramid with the agility of a graceful antelope, he was none other than my brother Hussein. He always recited this poetic verse: "Knowledge raises a house that has no pillars. Ignorance lowers the house of glory and honor." Then he would descend quickly before the necks of the senior students, who were lifting him, snapped. And when the guest visited the classes, I was often called to recite some lessons or famous essays of wisdom.

When Teachers Abstain

The first official report issued in 1950 on "The Conditions of Education in the Emirate of Bahrain" stated that the number of Bahraini male and female students in 1943 was 2,253 male and female students and that the education budget at that time was 243,000 Indian rupees. The report also indicated that the Department of Education was finding it difficult to provide teachers, either locals or delegates from abroad on special contracts, and that the teaching profession did not become regulated until after the arrival of the first Egyptian scholarship in 1944.

I was in the third grade there, and it was the last grade of primary school. Among the first Egyptian teachers was Mr. Sobhi Dahleh, a sarcastic teacher who never missed a joke or a wink. Mr. Youssef Al-Shirawi took on the task of organizing and promoting the much-welcomed sarcastic bywords of this professor, just as he used to organize a funny reception for our teacher, Mr. Nayer, upon his entrance into the classroom.

Mr. Sobhi, in our class, utilized a new method for memorizing arithmetic lessons. Hence, he printed out about a hundred questions for us from the arithmetic course before the end of the year and promised that the questions of the final exam would be among them. Thus, the students ensured success in the subject, and the school ensured that the students absorbed the course material.

In contrast to Mr. Sobhi, Mr. Abdullah Abd al-Ahad al-Baydawi from Lebanon, who taught the subjects of Arabic and composition, was known for his eloquence and his admirable way of speaking, taking matters seriously and simply and spontaneously believing everything he was told. He would command me to put an "idle mark" for the student who exceeded the limit in actions or speech or was neglectful of the lesson, then the score would be deducted from the student's marks according to the number of marks, and I would hide for fear of the students' revenge.

One of the Egyptian teachers was the teacher of Arabic and rhetoric, Mr. Mahmoud Abdel-Ghani. When he first arrived at our school, he would follow the lesson with a lecture about Egypt and its splendor and beauty, and he would say that Egypt is the mother of the world, the heart of the Arab world, and the land of the Kanaan tribe in Palestine. The connection of the people of Bahrain with the Egyptian culture, the press, and the Al-Azhar establishment and their follow-up to the political events in Egypt were well known by most Bahrainis. It seemed as if the honorable professor stopped this propaganda when he saw the extent to which the people of Bahrain realized the beauty of Egypt and the extent of the love and appreciation they had for the country.

As for the Physical Education teacher Kamal Abdo, he was surprised when he first got here at the students' wearing the *dishdasha*, which he called "pajamas" and insisted on replacing it in the sports lesson with shirts and shorts, and he also tried—as a boxer—to establish boxing lessons and even bought, for that purpose, a set of leather gloves and tried to teach us. I tried boxing once, and then I left, if only just to save my nose and eyes!

During his reign, teams were formed for sports performances, matches, athletics, jumping, distance running, cycling, etc., and the champion of high jumping with a stick was Mr. Youssef Al-Shirawi. The runner who won the race in first place was my brother Hussein.

The Director of Education at that time, Mr. Wakelin, did not hesitate to fill the empty classes after the resignation of some teachers and the travel of others. He taught us our first-level science lessons in English in a dark basement room. He explained to us patiently while he was sweating from the intense heat in the room from having no ventilation or electric fan, and he would grab the snowflakes that would promptly melt before he could complete the explanation of the properties of water.

Mr. Wakelin was interested in developing teaching methods, especially when it came to teaching in the English language, so he introduced the basic language system in English. Our English teacher, Mr. Abul Qassim Faydhi, took over teaching English, and he had a high moral character and amazing patience in bearing the students' quarrels and mischief. One of said students used to anger teachers by entering their classrooms through the window instead of the door! Mr. Faydhi's insistence on communicating in English only helped us to raise our skill level in the English language a lot, but he quit teaching after it was rumored that he was preaching the Baha'i faith, and then he left Bahrain altogether.

The personalities of these teachers left their imprints in guiding the youth, and a number of these students made shining contributions in the social and cultural fields, especially in the celebrations of the Prophet's birthday and the Israa'i, i.e., *flaying to Jerusalem mosque,* and *Mi'raj*, i.e., flaying to heaven.

A monthly magazine was issued by the name of the Secondary School Revelation, a public library was established in the school, and its students represented the novel (for the sake of the crown).

Mr. Al-Arrayed and the Twinkling Stars

The sky is a world in itself, with its beauty and far-distanced stars. However, perhaps few people are used to looking at the sky on a dark night to enjoy its charm or to keep pace with its shining, flowering stars that gleam in its paths, permeable even in the darkness of the night, or hidden in the shyness of a shining moon. In this sense, Abu Al-Ala Al-Ma'arri (a famous blind Arab poet) praised the guidance of his insight and the transparency of his spirit when he said:

"Sometimes a dark night becomes so beautiful like a shining morning, even if it is dressed in black.

It is as if I said that the full moon is a child, and the youth of darkness are in a state of violence.

My night is a Negro bride with necklaces of *Juman* (i.e., a precious glimmering stone).

As the crescent moon loves the Pleiades, they embrace each other in farewell.

Sohail (a star in the constellation Argo Navies, also referred to as Canopus) has the red cheek of a beloved and the heartbeat of a lover.

Twinkling with red so quickly, as if it were the eye of one irate.

His feet behind him, and he is in his disability, like a courier, without feet."

Undoubtedly, poets, philosophers, and lovers alike are among those who admire the beauty of the sky. As for astronomers, they observe the celestial bodies in a concrete, scientific way, not really appreciating their poetic allure.

During my secondary school studies, I fell in love with the world of the sky and the path of the stars. Behind that was our great professor, the poet Ibrahim Al-Arrayed, and it is not right to talk about secondary school without praising our famous professor, who combined in his passion for the stars the effort of the scientist, the meditation of the philosopher, and the feelings of the delicate poet.

Before his class, all I knew of the stars was the polar star, and, in vain, my classmate Abdul Aziz Al-Qadi tried to introduce me to the planets and other stars, but he did not succeed. And I continued as such until Professor Al-Arayid came to work at our secondary school as a substitute teacher on loan; thus, I benefited greatly from his explanation about the expanse of the sky. Furthermore, Al-Arrayed's lessons would not end when the time expired; I would always ask him, and he would always help me, wherever I met him. He liked his students, and they liked him from the very first lesson he gave, as if they had all been previously acquainted with him. He began teaching mathematics in English, but it was not difficult for most students to understand it thanks to his teaching method.

I loved theoretical geometry very much, and I was fond of the logical assumptions and proofs laid down by the Greek philosophers. Thus, I was the first in the class to learn new lessons by myself before they were due, even if the geometry lesson happened in the afternoon and our stomachs were still full, so I would start yawning. The class students followed me, yawning or pretending to do so. Mr. Arrayed could not stop himself from yawning as well. So he got angry at me and gave me the choice between leaving the class or moving to the back. So I did the later. And I do not recall ever yawning in his class again. I had heard Mr. Al-Arrayed's previous students talk about him before he came to teach at our school. They said that in spite of his far-reaching patience, he did not tolerate, with people, dullness of misunderstanding, foolishness, frozen feeling, ridiculousness questions, and wandering of the mind. They also said that if he got angry, he would show you the stars of the sky at noon! This is an Arabic idiom to describe intense anger.

Mr. Ibrahim Al-Arrayed's nickname in Bahrain was Al-Ustadh Al-Arrayed (*al-ustadh* means "the Professor"). I was pleased to be popular with Al-Ustadh Al-Arrayed when he said, "Oh, my son, you must see the stars in the sky in the darkness of the night at varying times in order to complete your knowledge of them." And he set an appointment for that during the school's trip to Budaiyi' in the spring season, and he himself accompanied me on these space trips, along with Mr. Saeed Tabbara, my brother Hussein, Hussein Mandeel, and other students. Their number decreased after that, because the first date with the stars was after the brightest dinner! The second date was late during sleep!

It was as if the stars of the sky were fluctuating in their positions, and the moving planets during the night refused to rise or disappear without a look of farewell or the hug of a meeting with their lovers. So, there was no wonder that our *Ustadh* took the trouble of getting up late at night and stumbled through the tents to wake us up from deep slumber after a day full of wandering and fatigue. Undoubtedly, every vigil was made easy in order to book an appointment at the end of the night with "a negro bride from amongst the *jinn*, who wore necklaces of *Juman, i.e., a famous precious stone*."

*

War and Seasons of Giving

With the beginning of the Second World War, people remembered the voice of the late Muhammad Dweiger announcing the opening of Bahrain Radio, the first radio station in the Gulf. I remember the voice of the late Mr. Salem al-Arrayed broadcasting a commentary on the eloquent speeches of Mr. Churchill. With the exception of the news bulletin and commentary on the news—both of which were considered an extension of London Arabic Radio—the audience eagerly followed the local and Arab news, literary talk, popular songs, and whatever else was playing on the radio. People were busy buying radios or improving the performance and appearance of their existing ones. The radio was not a common commodity found in every home, so visiting neighbors to listen to the radio was a common pastime during the war, just as later became the situation with the television set, which was in its infancy.

The owner of the radio set would usually choose which broadcast to listen to, and the other listeners would surrender to this choice, whether it was the program "This is London," or "This is Berlin," or "This is Bahrain." The Berlin Radio and its hero, Younes Bahri, was a broadcast that was mixed with caution because Bahrain Government Adviser Mr. Belgrave had issued an order prohibiting listening to Berlin Radio. Accordingly, the volume of the radio was turned down, so guests who listened would approach the radio with their ears wide open, and the intensity of their attention would increase, so they would gather around the radio as if they were preparing to devour a stuffed sheep, so that anyone who accidentally coughed would feel a sense of embarrassment, as his fellow listeners may have missed important news about the encroachment of Rommel over the Western Sahara in Libya or of the Germans seizing an important position.

Soon after, the commentary phase would begin, right after the news bulletin, and each of them would analyze the news according to his own personal understanding and feelings, and the voices would intermingle in a mixture of the smoke of *gadoo* (smoking shisha) and *oud* (burning incense). Those brazen voices and heightened emotions would not subside until a second news bulletin started or until they heard the voice of one of the locals who had become famous for relating and analyzing the current news, marking his arrival at the *majlis* (gathering). He would usually be a person who specialized in constant listening to the radio, reading newspapers and magazines, and wandering between listening councils by night and offices and markets by day. From among them, I knew the late Muhammad Saleh Al-Shirawi and Mr. Mustafa Al-Alawi, as well as Mr. Youssef Zulaikh. What I heard about the latter was that he would knock on people's doors in the middle of the night whenever he got wind of breaking news, as he could not force himself to be patient and wait until morning came. When the night guards questioned him, he would claim that he was searching for a runaway goat!

As for the one who had missed one of the nightly gatherings, he was able to satisfy his thirst for news from the newspaper "Al Bahrain" of the late Abdullah Al-Zayid, as he took his time to read a whole page about "A Hadith Broadcasted from Bahrain Station Yesterday." If his eyes did not become tired of the small, rough-printed letters and the faded colors of the poor-quality paper, he would continue to read the rest of the pages filled with news, poetry, and literature. And his eyes would inevitably fall on a side of the literary battles that were raging at that time between Ibn Al-Amid, Ibn Al-Roumi, and other writers.

I would not have understood much at the time about these literary battles had it not been for what I heard about them afterward, as it seemed to me that most of them were echoes of the famous literary battles on the pages of Egyptian newspapers that raged between famous writers such as Al-Akkad, Al-Mazini, Taha Hussein, Al-Rafi'i, Zaki Mubarak, and others.

I was interested in Bahrain Radio for reasons other than the news bulletin. The late Ahmed Yateem was busy with acting on the radio, and he invited me with my brother and Abdulaziz Al-Qadi to participate in acting, as I was allowed to imitate the soft voices of ladies. Perhaps the charade that I participated in was the first on the radio, and its title was "Kisra of Persia and the Arabs." We rehearsed for it at the Ahlia school of Mr. Altajir. Then we moved to the house of Abd Allah Bashmi, and Rashid Qaratah joined us. The training was not limited to memorizing our roles and perfecting our performance, but rather, the creation of sound effects took up most of the time. Ahmed Yateem was so busy coming and going throughout the period of practices, along with bringing what he could of the house and kitchen tools to imitate the sound of horses' hooves, fencing, the outbreak of war, and so on. The live broadcast would be on the air; thus, it would require perfection, avoiding mistakes, and silencing one's breath! Soon after that, the cultural clubs took the initiative to go down to the audience on stage. The theaters were not well prepared in terms of decor, lighting, and audiovisual effects, but they performed their role successfully and attracted a large audience of people. It was strange that when the theaters were organized after that and were coming very close to brilliance, they lost their huge audience.

Then the flame of the plays died down, and the clubs became dominated by the lottery, power show parties, weightlifting, and then to the "Housey Housey= TAMBOLA" games for the sake of improving their income.

**

= 6 =
Me and the Orouba Club
Nadi Al-Orouba

*

In 1939, a new cultural club was established in Manama, near and on the same road of my secondary school. I was nine years old at the time.

I admired this club, which was devoted to promoting the education, knowledge, and guidance of the young generation.

I was not a member of the Orouba club at that time, but that did not prevent me from visiting the club, reading their newspapers, borrowing their books in disguise (under the name of one of the club's members) to read at home, and attending compelling literary club events. The halls in the club were customarily crowded with dignitaries, professors, and distinguished public figures who were motivated by their appreciation or curiosity.

The late president of the club, Muhammad Dowaiger, usually opened these cultural speeches by giving advice in a somber radio broadcaster style and stressing the importance of morals in promoting the renaissance of nations and of the duties of the youth and teachers toward society. On a side note, Mr. Dowaiger was the director and main speaker of the Bahrain radio station during World War II. He would soon be followed by the Secretary, Ustadh Hassan Al-Jishi. His elaborate style and his ideas opposing stagnation, calling for development and openness to the broader concept of Arabism, contributed to raising the degree of enthusiasm among some of his audience as well as the tension of nerves among others. And if it happened that he was followed next by the speech of the Ustadh Ali Altajir, the attendees would then imagine that they were facing a lava-spewing volcano as a result of frank dialogue, stinging criticism, and bursts of enthusiasm like a stormy wave covered by a wave above it, a wave greater than it. And as the shocks continued, the stunned mouths would widen and would remain that way until the end of his speech. Then the party hosts would try smoothing the atmosphere with a break for refreshments or a romantic poem from among the poetry of the late Mr. Al-Sayyid Radhi Al-Mousawi, such as this one:

"Spread flowers over the page of eternity, whose winds radiate perfume at sunrise."

Hassan Al-Jishi and Al-Mousawii were well-known in the community. The first was a famous speaker, and the second was a well-known poet. As for Mr. Ali Altajir, it was not known about him that he used to write poetry as well. Had it not been for what the Orouba Club parties had recorded, I would not have known. What I found recorded from one of these occasions was his poetry in the year 1360 AH (1940), which read as follows:

"We are lost in a wasteland where events attack us by,

A traitorous intruder.

Unarmed, we have no power to defend ourselves.

Submissive, no ambition for challenges of glory,

We respond with bitter submission.

The ember of religion has died out in our hearts.

Our minds got lost in the crusts.

The fathers faded away; the light vanished,

In a bed of darkness.

Ah, if life could but revive its light in our souls and hearts, then we could make this life as blissful as Paradise.

And then we could reveal life secrets openly, out in the sunlight."

*

Literary participation was not limited to club members, as a number of Bahraini writers, poets, headmasters, and teachers from educational missions participated in it from time to time. The commentary and discussion would also be undertaken by the eminent scholars of religion and the guests present.

The great professor and poet, Ibrahim Al-Arrayed, was the brilliant star illuminating most of the club's parties. Entire evenings were devoted to him and were spent reciting his new anecdotal poetry, fraught with admiration and applause from those present. Between 1940 and 1943, he recited a number of his poems, such as "Two Kisses," "The Living Statue," "The Twins," "The Legend of Omar Alkhayam," "The Heart of a Dancer," and others.

*

I would eagerly keep up with the club's cultural evenings and attend them, so I would sit—as a young boy—behind the rows, crammed into the back corner, and no one cared about my presence! But I dared to stand up from time to time to follow the expressive movements of Professor Al-Arrayed. One movement of his arm knocked the glass of water off of his podium and spilled water all over the podium and his official robe. I could not resist the urge to laugh. Nothing could disturb my delight except my anxiety about returning home late and walking alone through the darkness, amongst the lonely alleyways, through which echoes of the frightful sounds of watchmen injured the silence and stillness of the night. As I wandered home, someone suddenly shouted from the end of the alley, "*Shint*?" (meaning, "Who are you?").

I answered him in a hoarse voice, filled with fear: "A friend!" I also had to answer to my father after that about my reason for being late.

*

Professor Al-Arrayed was my teacher for a period of time during my secondary school. I envied him for all the love and admiration he received from the club.

Time passed, so that the student who had been keen to attend the club's parties and had resorted to borrowing books in the name of actual members would become an official club member. I was one of said students who was granted membership. Further, I was entrusted once with being the director of the library, so I would quickly busy myself in arranging books in order to write a report on all of them and submit it to the Board of Directors. I wrote another report, also, regarding books that needed to be banned and multiple reports about books borrowed by members and not returned by them, etc.

This kind of work gave me a sense of happiness and contentment, because it is what put me face to face with the references and classic books that I had heard of from my teachers at school or through listening to lectures or through my reading, such as the historical works of al-Tabari and Subh Al-A'sha, as well as dictionaries, famous authors and historians, and the four books of literature: Al-Aghani, Al-Aqd Al-Farid, Amali, and Al-qali, along with the encyclopedia of Wajdi's Al Ma'arif and others. The system would prevent the borrowing of reference books, so I attempted to read all of them at the club itself.

Moreover, the work of organizing the library would hardly reach an end before it would start anew. It was the custom of the veteran members that most of them started their visit to the club by entering the library and wandering along its open shelves, then not leaving the room until after tampering with some of the books and references. They would leave the books in any place in a hurry, rushing to the sitting room to read the newspapers. It was as if by doing this they satisfied their arrogance or their sense of curiosity, or that they showed the new members a characteristic of intellectual interest that distinguished them from all the rest.

*

Observant Look at the Club

The club had an old yet solid gate with two shutters, worn out at the ends, especially on the lower parts where the two shutters met the corroded door stop, from which an opening in the form of a small crescent allowed the movement of rats to and fro.

A thick wood board rose above the gate with the name of the club written on it, and below it was the name of its writer, the calligrapher Ahmed Al-Othman, in very clear print.

The one entering the club would find himself in a small, semi-dark vestibule that ended with an opening from the left overlooking a rectangular open courtyard that led from the west to the main rectangular room that was used for sitting, reading, holding public parties, and some administrative work as well. Then, from the south, it is connected to the library room. There was a third room with solid walls along the corridor, with only a door overlooking the courtyard from the west.

I mentioned the main rectangular room in which the parties were held, and I do not recall anything more than that, except that it was the most beautiful room in the club, and it was so long that it could accommodate the huge crowd that typically gathered each day to read the newspapers, along with those who would sit to talk or to have refreshments, and for those who performed administrative work. At times, it even entertained another group of intellectuals, who used to hold discussions and flex their muscles of thought or gather to share knowledge with one another in the fields of poetry, literature, history, and so on, where classical and colloquial styles were mixed, and all of the above was mixed with words and terms in English.

If you were sitting amongst them reading a newspaper, with your nose buried in the paper, not raising your head to take in what was happening around you, and you heard a loud, anxious-sounding voice that had a sort of musical tone to it, then you could be sure that that was the voice of the club secretary, Mr. Hassan Al-Jishi. But if you heard huge sentences, most of which ended with the English word "humbug," you would know with certainty that the speaker was Mr. Ali Altajir. As for Professor Ibrahim Al-Arrayed's voice and tone, they were distinctive to most of the members because of his calm, caring, and gentle style that was typically interspersed with the phrase, "My son." The professor rarely got angry. However, if he did, we would hear the roar of a lion, and whoever was arguing with him would instantly fall silent!

The members of the Board of Directors frequently argued and quarreled, especially on the topic of how to spend the club funds.

Sometimes, some of clergymen come to visit the club, and their luck puts them in the way of one of the members while entering the club, so he invites them to the club to be faced with criticism concerning illiberal religious beliefs.

Among the scholars who enjoyed special appreciation and respect from those members was the late Sheikh Abdul-Hussein Al-Hilly (head of the religious court), as his ideas were young, lively, and vigorous, and the members liked that. Among the other scholars I will mention is His Eminence, the late Sheikh Abdullah Muhammad Saleh. He was shown great respect whenever he visited the club. This, however, did not prevent the members from crossing the line with him in freedom of speech, so that opinions would clash and voices would be raised!

*

At the entrance to the library room overlooking the courtyard on its side was a long bench of stone built for sitting, but no one was interested in sitting on it, as it was one of the remnants of the *majlis* of the late Sheikh Khalaf Al-Usfoor, who was the previous owner of the building, which was used by him as a *majlis* in which to receive his guests.

As for that dark room that I mentioned, which was the third room—I was afraid to enter it while I was a student, but when I became a member of the club and was entrusted to reopen the education branch, I was nominated by the club to teach students in that room as there was no other place in the club but this one. What remains in my memory of it was three things—the first: that the room's floor was dusty, and the second: that the "blackboard" was not easily run over by chalk due to its roughness and the cracks that covered it, and the third: the education lasted for a year or more, then the students dispersed, only one of them remaining. He continued alone for about a month while I was waiting in the reading room. I would become aware of his arrival from the sound of his loose shoes pulling across the ground. He was a young man from the outskirts of Manama. One night I did not hear the sound of his walking, and I waited for a long time, but he did not show up. So we closed that branch.

Furthermore, as you climbed, albeit with some difficulty, the steep stair steps to reach the rooms upstairs, you would hear some commotion and shouting from the rooftop room designated for practicing indoor games. The first person who would usually confront you in this room was Mr. Ali Altajir and Mr. Abbas Al-Alawi in their eternal struggle over the game of backgammon. And they played it with skill and speed. This still did not prevent one or both of them from participating in the transmission of news, encouraging players, or challenging those who played against them.

Mr. Ali Altajir used to hold his discussions in the sitting room, but they were not complete until this opportunity arose, as he then had the chance to argue with a crowd of members while he was playing, so he would turn to each of them separately until he was silenced by the word "*taq,*" then he would return to the next player, and so on. The topics of the hour were often controversial, such as King Farouk and the parties of Egypt, the news and the events of Palestine, and Nuri al-Saeed of Iraq and his proposal to form the Fertile Crescent between Iraq, Jordan, Syria, and perhaps Lebanon. This proposal was rejected by Jamal Abdul Naser of Egypt and other Arab countries who supported him as being a colonial British plan. If the political events were exhausted, there was also discussion about the true concept of religion and support for the opinions of the Egyptian Al-Ansar magazine on Arabism and Islam, and so on.

Mr. Ali used to play chess sometimes, and I learned how to play for his sake. As for the others in the game room, you could find them often busy playing checkers or dominoes, but the favorite game of the club's fans was *carom* table, a game that most board game players do not usually like, including Mr. Ali Altajir, because of the noise and loud commentary that always accompanied its gameplay. It would give the club management a chronic headache, because of which Mr. Ali resigned from the club until he was persuaded to rescind his resignation. Another activity in the rooftop rooms took place in another room, which was divided into two parts: one half was the administrative office, and the other part was dedicated to the tennis table, at which I enjoyed playing. The remaining area on the rooftop was used for hosting cultural activities during the summer months in place of the designated room on the ground floor.

The heat on the club's rooftop was harsh on members in the afternoons and evenings alike. But, in spite of that, it witnessed frequent cultural lessons, discussions, and debates, as well as the weekly and monthly internal lectures. It also witnessed the beginning of training for stage plays—internal and external—for the radio station and the public.

Most of the speakers in those internal parties would usually start their speeches by belittling themselves in the wording and exaggerating the slander of their poor ideas and ill thoughts, and they might refer to themselves with humble words, despicable according to the customs of their fathers, and then conclude that preamble by saying that he agreed to participate to satisfy insistence from the secretary or head of the club, and then and only then would he start reading his papers.

Members did not want to miss attending those evenings, especially if the program included something exciting, such as competitions, prizes, acting, music, or singing, as well as for the purpose of showing generosity in hospitality in the presence of an outside well-known visitor, but the number of attendees was far less when the party was limited to listening to written speech written or quoted words. In which case, the attendees seemed to become bored, and they would show this by absent-mindedness, fidgeting while sitting, or audibly yawning... All of these things would cause the secretary to become embarrassed.

Clubs in Bahrain were instructed, by law, not to indulge in politics or religious affairs, yet on one evening I witnessed at Al-Orouba Club the signing of a petition to the ruler of Bahrain, Sh. Salman bin Hamad al-Khalifa, by some activists, headed by Mr. Abdulrahman Al-Baker, for political reforms.

Picnics: One of My Favorite Memories

Al-Orouba Club had been organizing recreational picnics for members to orchards, sea beaches, and islands, especially the island of "Al-Nabi Saleh," before its connection to the mainland, to Sitra Island, when its only outlet was the bridge set up by the oil company "Bapco," also to the island of "Umm Al-Naasan" and the orchard of His Highness the Amir in Al-Wasmiya, as well as other parks and orchards. The season of most of these trips was during the hot summer months, and their timing was on the weekend. The participants enjoyed sleeping on the sandy beaches of the islands or in the orchards. Then, on Friday morning, they rushed to the natural springs, such as Ain al-Rahi and the Safaniyah. Where there were no natural springs, there were artesian wells in orchards and traditional swimming pools, and around them were some old buildings and their facilities. As for the areas with natural springs, there were no buildings around them, and the shades of palm trees and other trees here and there were the only refuge from the glare of the sun. The return time was usually Friday evening. Night may fall during the return if one of the boats malfunctioned on the way, or if the captain lost his way.

Going on excursions of this kind to these places was a common activity in Bahrain. Those recreational trips had social, psychological, and emotional connotations that caused them to occupy a large space in the record of my memories.

I had observed the educated and experienced members of the club on those trips, and I found most of them were incapable of relying on themselves and less able to help others, except in issuing orders. A number of uneducated people, or simple-minded people, were admired in those circumstances and had the authority and experience that it took to run the affairs of those trips.

Moreover, you would find that such people were characterized by simplicity and kindness, and they were more aware of the windings of the roads, and had a deeper knowledge of the places and people, and were able to deal with them. They often came to the rescue on those trips, motivated by the love of helping others.

As soon as the backpackers landed, you would see them working like busy bees, preparing meals and distributing refreshments. Then you would find amongst them someone who spread the ground, someone who transported water, someone who cooked, someone who started the campfire, and someone who poured cups of coffee and tea. And they would meet people with a bright face, smiling and happy with what they had done. It is as if, until now, I can hear the laughter and jokes of the late Jaafar Al-Nasser, and I can see clearly the smile of the late Noah Qassem and his happiness every time I addressed him with jokes because of his name, saying, "Where is the ship, Noah?" It is as if I were in the presence of the late Sayyed Abbas Al-Alawi, exchanging roles with others like Rashid Al-Mahouzi, Radhi Al-Qumish, Abdullah Al-Watani, the late Ayoub Hussein, and Kazem Al-Asfoor. Even if the table was set and the meal was served, I always found them to be the happiest people, the least greedy, the most patient in terms of humor, and the most patient in terms of criticism.

On these recreational trips, club members—young and old—mixed, and some of them would venture out with their parents, siblings, or relatives, so they would coexist, despite the differences between them, as a small community. And in situations such as those, when the people of determination and enthusiasm showed their brothers the best of their human talents, what they would hear of words of appreciation and admiration provided them with psychological compensation that filled them with satisfaction and happiness, and the club reaped a lot of benefits from it all!

= 7 =
Back to My Secondary School

*

Literary Agreement to Twenty Articles

Abdulaziz Muhammad Al-Qadi was my classmate. His family was very well known in Saudi Arabia. He was a good poet and a master of the Arabic language.

He proposed to me the idea of meeting up with him to exchange our ideas on the subjects of culture, knowledge, literature, poetry, and the like. He emphasized that this was a serious endeavor and required a signed agreement between us stating, "We, the two undersigned, have resolved, with God's help, to exchange opinions and ideas that include scientific, literary, and social aspects, which will bring us the hoped-for benefit," etc…Then this introduction would be followed by organizing how to cooperate on writing twenty articles! It was most likely during the year 1943 AD, when I was thirteen years old. We started our dialogue on those matters. We exchanged, for a period of time, opinions and research that included poetry, literature, philosophy, morals, customs, philology, the meaning of happiness, and so on. Then he insisted—according to our agreement—on copying down minutes of all meetings and making a full report, recording the position of each party with regard to what we agreed on and on which ideas we had differing opinions.

Once, he authored a very good poem about a shining moon and asked me to challenge him in writing my own. But my poetry was so weak that he laughed, criticizing my poetry skills. I had expected this response from him, knowing that—in addition to the age difference between us—he had a solid literary talent.

After a year or longer of conversations and debates, agreement and disagreement, boredom descended on the two young souls yearning for knowledge and looking forward to completing their studies, and the agreement slipped into the corner of oblivion. There had been a new element that appeared on the scene that had captured attention of them both. It was the Cairo *Al-Ansar* magazine, the *Arab Ideology and Islamic Culture* issue.

**

= 8 =
About the Al-Ansar Movement and Its Magazine in (Cairo-Egypt)

*

In 1939, during the start of World War II, a group was formed in Cairo to promote Arabism and Islamic ideology, wherein they began calling for meetings with official personalities and intellectuals. They also published a monthly magazine under the name of *Al-Ansar*. The official license was in the name of Hassan Abdul Maqsood, and the Chief Editor was Sheikh Ahmed Sabry Shuwaiman, who was the sole owner and writer in it.

In his last article in the Cairo *Al-Ansar* magazine in the year 1363 AH (1944 A.D.), Ahmed Sabry announced the end of *Al-Ansar* and that this magazine would cease to be published. Before it finally stopped being published, he explained the history of the movement and the beginning of its formation, as it was the effort of a few devoted individuals toward the idea of *Al-Ansar* being "in compliance with the boundaries and restrictions—invisible, not audible, nor dangerous. And they were a group in Egypt of no more than eleven men." The onset was in the year 1359 AH, when the Islamic societies in Egypt held three meetings of a general conference with the aim of reaching an "Islamic front," where about 60 societies attended these meetings! But they all ended in failure because of hatred, intense competition for the presidency and positions, and disagreement over wording, as well as exchanges of sparkling words! Ahmed Sabry witnessed these meetings and ascertained to him their futility, so he established a "Cultural Guidance" body, with the basis of its work being to bring the true Islamic culture closer to the minds of the intellectuals, that the foundation of its law would mean the abolition of the presidential system, and that the number of the group would not exceed 25, as well as that the well-known writers and writers whose unaccepted inclinations and goals were defined would not be permitted to join. Then well-known names, such as Hassan Abdel-Maqsoud, editor of Al-Ahram newspaper; Mohamed Mohyi El-Din, professor of architecture at the Higher Institute of Arts; Mohamed Abu Bakr Ibrahim, inspector of the Arabic language at the Ministry of Education; and a poet who was not mentioned, joined this body. and a number of educators at the university, the House of Science, and other cultural bodies, including:

Hamed Abdel Qader, Professor of Psychology and Semitic Languages at Dar Al Uloom, Dr. Ahmed Fikri, and two well-known journalists. The Ansar Council then reached eleven members.

Then *Al-Ansar* magazine was issued to take on the form of this cultural guidance, and the messages of Al-Ansar were the material and reference for this guidance; and from those messages were issued the book "Scientific Theories in the Qur'an," then "The Pharaonic Mask," then "Light in the History of the Unity of God."

As for the magazine itself, Ahmed Sabry distanced himself from the directives of the commission and its council so that there would be no quarrels, and Hassan Abdel-Maqsoud was satisfied with the privilege of being the holder of the official license of the magazine. The *Al-Ansar* family held three acquaintance parties in three successive years, which were witnessed by many personal friends. The owner of *Al-Ansar* describes them as an elite of men known in society for their honesty and cultural efforts. With these meetings alone—although it was no more than a frivolous display—the supporters frightened many of their staunch enemies. Ahmed Sabry says, in discussing the story of the inception of the magazine, "Everything around us in the year 1359 AH (1939 A.D.) was as it is today, being similar to the Tower of Babel. However, the biggest reform step we took during the first year was to paralyze the movement of those scholars with qualifications who aspired to benefit from a modern reform wave such as *Al-Ansar*, wherein determination and wit served a definitive goal in the form of a lively magazine. So, their intensity gradually eased until they moved from founders in the *Al-Ansar* movement to persevering contributors in reading it, swearing allegiance to its activity, and aiding it from the point of view of their influence as much as possible."

After about a year of the cultural body meetings, it became lost in discussions and suggestions, and the magazine was published. Some of its articles contained research on the Pharaonic era and on the campaign against the famous Taha Hussein and his policy "in the unknowns of the Ministry of Education," which upset the friends of the supporters' scholars, along with the clergymen of art, experts of the Arabic language, and other intellectual figures.

Nonetheless, *Al-Ansar* continued its march against the current for four years with the pens of its not-so-popular writers. The well-known pens were limited to a few names and articles, including Muhammad Saeed Al-Arian, Muhib Al-Din Al-Khatib, Farid Al-Rawi, Muhammad Mohi Al-Din, then Fahd Al-Rimawi, Muhammad Asaad Rajeh, and the owner of the license, Hassan Abdel-Maqsood, as if the magazine was abandoning those well-known names, or they were abandoning at least one at the beginning of each year, until their writers became limited to those three last names stated above.

Al-Ansar and the Setting Sun

"Palaces rise and fall, high-rise skyscrapers rise and then collapse, but the edifices of countries that the Arabs built in the name of God dozens of times are not like palaces and edifices. On earth are the ruins of religion, not the ruins of the kingdoms, and the evidence of justice, not the remnants of tyranny, and together there have been consciousness, comfort, and prosperity, not traces of humiliation, submission, and fear. Humanity will cry a lot in these ruins and will mourn for long at these memories of ruins!"

Those are the words of Ahmed Sabry, the owner of *Al-Ansar*, the magazine which is our subject of focus in this chapter.

Al-Ansar had supporters and followers in countries outside of Egypt, such as Syria, Lebanon, Jordan, Iraq, Yemen, and Bahrain.

In Bahrain, *Al-Ansar* attracted a number of intellectuals, poets, and school teachers and students.

The famous poet in Bahrain, Ustadh Ibrahim Al-Orayyed, sent a heart-touching poem to *Al-Ansar*, and so did my classmate Abdul Azzi Al-Qadi, as well as my secondary school mate Sheikh Khalid bin Mohamed Al-Khalifa. I followed suit when I was 14 years old and sent in my own poetry. Other followers in Iraq, Syria, Jordan, and Oman participated in Al-Ansar, too, sending in what they had authored of articles and poems. Egyptians and others were proud of the history of the Pharaonic dynasty. Ahmed Sabry of *Al-Ansar* had another revolutionary idea toward this matter. He was criticized in Egypt for printing a book about the Pharaonic civilization.

We read in his book "The Mask of Pharaonic" the following passage about the Pharaonic civilization of Egypt: "Indeed, the ancient Egyptians, in the era of the Pharaohs, were strong but were composed of two elements: one of them was their servitude to their lords, and the other was their ignorance of civil rights. Their submission and oppressed strength were more like the extraction of oil juice—you will find at the end the pressure of a pressing mill and an obedient bull. He removed the mask of the face of the Pharaohs and described in detail the slavery of the Egyptians and the murder of the disobedient, as well as the Jews, the slavery of women, and using force and oppression against humanity and human rights."

Further, for those who inquired about the reality of the conditions of the Arabs and Muslims in this era, he answers: "Now, after a thousand and some hundreds of years, Arabs and Muslims are returning to their small homelands, to poverty of resources and poverty of living."

Al-Ansar and the New Ideology

We read in *Al-Ansar* magazine this preface: "Islam and Arab culture, as people should realize with a sense of understanding and conviction, require in this era to be presented with faith in them in a correct way, based on science, logic, and recognition of all the developments in which people's knowledge has expanded in the recent times, and the mental persuasion that most of what has come out of these illusions of development is idle talk from the overview of the advancement of humanity and a mistake in the wrong direction for humanity in general and for the Muslims in particular." In another excerpt, it said: "Knowledge in this era has made it possible for Europe's one-eyed ill-sight to have an inside look into our history, our conditions, and the secrets of our renaissance; thus, this history must help us, as Arabs ourselves, and by using the same knowledge and tools, to respond to this ourselves by exploring the East and West together."

We have, in our grasp, sufficient means to investigate historical events, ripples of the minds, differences in faith and beliefs, and the conflict of desires that make us able, by way of comparison of experience, to extract our own conclusions with regard to behavioral conduct and various belief systems.

Through this method, we see differences and conflicts between countries and nations, while our lives, our future, and our fate are tied to them. Our co-existence with these nations is mandatory in the form of mutual benefits and communication in this one human body that we cannot separate ourselves from, including its borders, its laws, and its commitments, as well as its future and destiny.

And we each see all of that from our own point of view.

*

As for the reason for this growing admiration, day after day, for the magazine and its topics and the anticipation of its new issues at the beginning of each *Hijri* month, it was a matter that was difficult to define and limit.

The truth was that *Al-Ansar* did everything in its power to explain and defend those ideas with rare boldness throughout the four years of its lifespan—ideas that were emerging from new horizons, starkly different from what the readers were familiar with in magazines or in the bellies of libraries, to the extent that many were puzzled in the classification of *Al-Ansar*, whether its ideas are progressive or reactionary. The magazine used to publish letters of both praise and criticism of *Al-Ansar* and provide for them straightforward replies. For instance, those who criticized *Al-Ansar's* ideas used to say things like what was published in *Alsabah* magazine in Damascus under the title "New School:" "This magazine is being edited by writers who are not yet famous yet who are confident in themselves, which invites you to revolt against the modern society—the "dark society," as they call it—and to return to a simple system of life and bestow lavishly upon their calls, discussions, and insults that they distribute amongst all people, along with references from science, argumentative force, and skillful in persuasion, because they are fighting the modern progressive life and they are familiar with all its intrusions."

*

Perhaps it would be best for me to stop for a while to introduce the writers of *Al-Ansar* magazine, their names, and the subjects of their writings, which is not an easy matter because of its brevity and prejudice.

1. Ahmed Sabry

We must start with the owner and the bearer of its idea, Ahmed Sabry Shuwaiman.

Among the writers in *Al-Ansar* magazine, Ahmed Sabry wrote the introduction of each issue under the name of "Hussam" and wrote under his name numerical articles to shed light on the history of monotheism in the life of the Arabs before Islam, and it became clear through his explanation that even though they were pagans on the surface, they were actually monotheists. These ideas fall under the theory of "the impact of environments on beliefs," as it indicates that the environment of the Arab desert in which the Bedouin lived led him to the knowledge of the essence of God.

He cited in support of this the opinions of previous thinkers, sociologists, and specialists in the study of the Arab migrations that emerged from the Arabian Peninsula, their history, and the characteristics of their social and mental lives. Because of this innate and moral willingness, God chose the Arab nation to carry the message of Islam, "and God knows where to place His message."

For this reason, the owner of *Al-Ansar* denounced what was rooted in the brains throughout history by the association of praise of Islam with vilification of the Arabs, belittling them and exaggerating the negative aspects that prevailed in their society before Islam, without paying attention to analyzing their origins and without proper investigation about the origin of this idea, which we believe was made up by hateful anti-Arab populists.

2. Mohamed Dhafer

Next, we meet another writer, Muhammad Dhafer, who was one of those aforementioned anonymous writers and whose permanent subject of writing was the of the title, "The Desired Islamic Society." He answered the question, "How would we live if we could imagine the continuation of the first Arab civilization period?" He criticized those who imagine the possibility of quoting the good of Western civilization without its evil because, as they have come to us today, they are inseparable. As for the correct action, it is to isolate scientific development from the cultures concurrent with it so that science and knowledge remain as general human heritage and we replace the imported cultures with our Arab Islamic culture. What is crucial is that knowledge and science remain, because no civilization in the world can advance without them. At the same time, we must use them according to our own needs and tastes. Our society then will not be a patchwork mixture, but rather our society will have an original, similar, and identical structure in it.

On another aspect of the desired Islamic society, Muhammad Dhafer discussed the economic factors in society and their impact on the roles of both men and women within it. He believed that the family system sheds light on the economic and financial systems and that the just Sharia law for women in Islam is neither about being veiled nor unveiled. And it is not about the technological advancement of tools and machines that have enslaved people, and it is not about scientific findings that have led to the oppression of nations. He also said, "Research into the family system has been put into the care of Islamic jurists who defend it with old arguments that are in their hands, on their tongues, and in their books. And the economic system, with all its issues and problems, has fallen out of their reach and attention because it appears to them there on the high foam in the choppy sea. But who can separate the family system from the rules of its social structure and its ideological guidance, as well as the economic laws that define the role of women in the fields of production, earning, and consumption, along with other rules that designate for women the correct ways of behaving in all aspects of their activity (in social and economic affairs)—taking, giving, and benefiting? The party who did separate family from economy and commercial life—Islamic preachers—instead chose to engage themselves repeatedly to continue unfinished discussions about the issues of rejecting the unveiling of women, the equality of women with men and its limits, the permissibility or denunciation of French dancing, the problem of women's clothing (a surface issue) and its solution, and whether it is permissible to marry four in this mechanical age or not. That is why economic affairs—with their contemporary terminology—have slipped by without Islamic public opinion discerning them, as if they, with all their strong influences, did not touch them at all!!"

3. Hamed Abu Al-Ataya
(another anonymous author)

Under the title, "Taking a Look at Our Mental Life," Hamed Abu Al-Ataya tackled the phenomenon of the poor quality and content of intellectual and cultural production in Arab society and stated that he considered the large proliferation of associations, clubs, and reform institutions, in their present form, a dangerous phenomenon that indicates the presence of the disease more than the availability of the medicine. He said that this was because the treatment was not within their reach. You find them wrestling with each other, whether for the sake of getting membership in the board of directors or for other desires and goals. They advertise for themselves in the yellow papers and magazines they print, begging for supporters, as if they were saying, "What do you like, reader? I want to satisfy your desires, so guide me to what you love and are satisfied with." Most books and magazines have now become like intense organic stimuli, no more or less. Thus, read a part of such-and-such book or spurn a topic from such-and-such magazine; it will help you—according to the experiences of those who know—to activate some glands or suppress some good human feelings!

Such yellow papers and the misguidance of those crippled societies must lead to mental separation from all moral responsibility, so that the reader becomes immersed in the world of amusement and the coma of bodily consumption. It is no wonder then that, with continued solicitation of readers to buy these magazines and books targeting the desires of readers in the first place—running after them, the same way that hunting dogs do—that our young readers have become addicted to the habit of buying those papers, even at times when they become bored with their written material. They buy it as a morning habit, read some titles in a hurry, and then toss it in the trash.

"What would you like, dear reader? I am at your disposal!" This is the language of the publisher, not the language of the thinker! Perhaps the thinkers have disappeared a long time ago… and the publishers have remained alone!

He also criticized the proliferation of reformist societies that do not get you fat and do not suffice you from hunger, where they are empty of mind, waiting for occasions to celebrate them, and they hold hollow meetings just for arguments with no results.

In such societies, a member is nothing more than a hollow name on a piece of paper, a number registered on a list, or a small amount of money he pays for his subscription each month, and he does not see any trace of it that appears other than in the lighting of the building, in paying some of the wages of employees and servants, or in buying a new mop for the shoes of those entering and leaving. He described the magazines issued by these associations as mute magazines!

4. Sadiq Al-Hakim (another anonymous writer)

As for the bearer of Al-Ansar's banner in the face of storytelling art, he was Sadiq al-Hakim. He confirmed that the art of storytelling was neither of Arab nor Islamic origin, and he skillfully tracked, with knowledgeable expertise, the origins of storytelling and theatrical art in the atmosphere of the Western society, where fog, cold, rain, and snow had an effect on the environment of people's lives and habits. It was not suitable for our society and did not fit with our thinking. For the Arabs, the story was limited to the good biography, the good example, the good work, and the heroism in the field of honors. And when Islam came, this meaning became firmly established through the Qur'anic miracles in the "best stories" and the most truthful ones. So, the stories in the Qur'an have become the lofty model that must be followed. Stories should become, in our part of the world, a tool for society building, not for demolition, and a source of awakening good feelings, not for numbing the senses!

"Art must return back to its nature. Nature, for the Arabs, gives birth to honest literature."

In conclusion, he said, "Nature, in Europe's geographical climate, with its freezing cold and snow throughout most of the year, evokes them to seek refuge in the fireplace, where storytelling becomes a form of compensation for the soul. On the other hand, Eastern nature, with its desert sunburn or green oasis, seeks refuge in fable storytellers."

In making a comparison between stories in the West and the East, he said:

"The story in Europe arose to achieve a general social purpose. Therefore, most stories and plays were a measure of political and social advancements in Europe. It was not a common occurrence that a political or social doctrine would spread in the great European countries, such as France, England, and Russia, before it was preceded by a narrative doctrine that paved the way for it for a long period of time. Behind most of idealistic movements, we find well-known writers and famous stories, as well as collecting its secrets and symbols."

He also said, "The icy, dark, and frightening nature of the West has become, in its essence, the subconscious minds of these peoples, from whom they derive hope in the art of compensating with stories and plays."

The writer affirms, at the end, that the art of storytelling in our part of the world, contrary to the West, is unable to carry the same task as in the West, where the story has become guidance for promoting ideological political and social reforms or making root changes in their society.

The story, in our lands, is subject to failure. Its main purpose is no more than to numb one's feelings and sense and to forget the sadness and suffering. That is the essence of story reading today.

5. Muhammad Asaad Rajeh (another anonymous writer)

The owner of *Al-Ansar*, Ahmed Sabry, gave way to Muhammad Asaad Rajeh to write about Sufism, so he wrote about the topic, dealing with it from a practical viewpoint in real life, citing the biographies of well-known Sufis, and denouncing the methods of deprivation and Sufi practices, to the extent that some of them even claimed to have been reincarnated!!

The owner of *Al-Ansar* did not forget to keep for himself various interventions on Sufism that were included in his articles, research, and responses in *Al-Ansar* magazine, issued from a comprehensive view of the meaning of Sufism and a broader and more distant conception. Rather, the importance that emerged in the subject of Sufism and its relevance to research in the history of monotheism compelled him to dedicate a special book for that under the name "Mysticism in the Perspectives of Islam: The Third Message of the Ansar," in which he explained the purpose of the book, writing:

"However, this comprehensive book, which *Al-Ansar* presents as a reference for Arab culture on the subject of Sufism, exceeds in its format and its far-reaching purposes the scope of those primary articles that we have prepared in the magazine for this research because this book does not revolve around the topics of Sufi figures and their conditions in the Islamic kingdoms. Rather, it comprehends the general reality of Sufism around the whole world and intends to explain it, clarify its ambiguities, and trace its components and manifestations amongst different peoples."

Then Ahmed Sabry summarized the definition of Sufism, in its various forms, as the severance of the means to reach God, then the illusion of reaching Him without actual reaching. Further, he stated that he believes that Sufism, in its comprehensive view, is a global behavior not limited by the limits of the partial methods and doctrines of which it consists. Moreover, he opined that it is a negative outlook on life that is characterized by standing at the means and forgetting the ends, and that Sufism is not limited to religion only but also transcends it to other aspects IN BOTH East and West nations. You will find in the West Sufism example under the theme of (art for art) and Sufism of the Bohemian movement, and now let us look to the ancient and modern times of the East and West and to the New World, where such beliefs overflow over all sects of human beings, and we will glimpse the effects of a Sufi movement that is expanding to both ends of the earth.

This perverted devotee of nature in the Far East is—in his eyes—the same eccentric dervish of the Middle and Near East, and he is the Bohemian, the horizontal, lurking with the most secrets, crossing the icy plains of Europe enveloped in its darkness.

From those restless souls who cannot relax or go back to the mainstream, thousands of images are flowing and emitted in Sufi behavior across time and space, bearing the same phases and the same ends. However, there is only one place on earth from which a Sufi has never emerged: it is the desert of the Arabian Peninsula.

Finally, Readers' Letters

Ahmed Sabry used to receive letters from the readers of *Al-Ansar* magazine. It was a platform from which he would conduct an intellectual dialogue with readers on various subjects. Some of them would give him criticism, to which he would reply in an explicit manner, whereas in other letters the readers would ask for more information and ideas. For example, one reader asked what he thinks regarding the well-known Muslim Brotherhood Movement in Egypt. He replied by giving full details about how this movement started under its leader Hassan Al-Banna in 1928, then he went back to discuss his personal life, when he was in Italy studying the art of sculpture, practicing in front of beautiful girl models. When he returned to Egypt after the Muslim Brotherhood movement, model girls suddenly disappeared, and in complete turn got him to call against woman freedom. Among the most prominent of these topics is the dispute over characteristics between the Arab and Aryan mentalities, as well as between the Semitic Arabs and Jews. We will quote an excerpt from that paragraph for the purpose of definition, which was published by *Al-Ansar* with the signature of "Hossam" from detailed research, which I personally consider as having been a prophecy in 1942. He said:

"We believe that the world's affairs, in their unification and complexity, and in their good and their evil, are a continuous exchange between the dominance of the sublime mentality with one of its two branches over it, namely the Arab mentality and the Jewish mentality. And this is clear to us Arabs as it is completely clear to the children of Israel! But this truth is still very far from the perceptions of those belonging to the Indo-European mentality, or the Aryan, or the non-Arabs at all, as we call it."

In the mail of the next issue of the magazine, *Al-Ansar* confirmed this belief by recording the following letter, from which we quote this paragraph:

"The world was divided in its influence between the message of the Arabs in religion and the message of the Jews in this world. And the world is witnessing, in this era, one of the fierce periodic battles between these two nations, and the two mentalities, and the two messages of sovereignty at the gates of Jerusalem, and all nations will recognize the extent of the great impact that the end of this violent conflict will have on the fate of the world. The Arabs are a small, upright nation, and the Jews are a small, misguided nation. The culture of each of them is widely spread in the world, so it is not lumped together in one place, and this means that the fate of the culture of the nations, in its good and its bad, is linked to this end, which everyone awaits with concern and awareness. Such concern we will find among those who are aware of the history of the world that its results will be greater than even the outcome of the more recent World War II. That is because the fate of Jerusalem, which is the great outer door to the House of God in Mecca as well as one of the main ports on the periphery of the homeland of monotheism in the Arab desert, will rule the world in the current of one of the two conflicting mentalities at the end of this conflict, so the world will go after the war into the abyss and Zionism or to security and Arabism!"

Al-Ansar and the Desert Migration

Meetings about *Al-Ansar* magazine occupied us for long periods, during which we would discuss the ideas of its writers, those who were known and those who were unknown. *Al-Ansar* magazine was serious about what it published. Its ideas—which it expressed boldly, frankly, and honestly—on various subjects were characterized by innovation and deviation from the postulates that were commonplace in society.

We used to meet in various places to discuss these ideas—at school, in the club, or in the market, but the most beautiful meetings by far were those that took place in the council of Sheikh Khalid bin Muhammad Al-Khalifa (a member of Bahrain's royal family), who was like a burning ember in his enthusiasm, frankness, and the strength of his might. And whether we are sitting with him in his reception room at the oasis of Alamer, where sand and dunes whispered and shadows and heat alternated under the shade of a wild tree near a spring of water around which camels and sheep circulated, or it was on a bench in the confines of the house, over which shade extended and the sun had begun to set. Or it was in another area in his garden at Albedaa, above the white sands at the edge of the seashore. Regardless of their whereabouts, the talks always started with *Al-Ansar* and then relaxed their ends to make way for talking about the desert and its news, as well as its poems and their narrators, while enjoying sipping of Arabic coffee and relaxation.

We also would sometimes meet in the Khalifiya Library in Muharraq, in the Majlis of the late Sheikh Ali bin Khalifa and his good sons in Muharraq, or on the coast of Al Jabour, opposite the Bahrain Fort. Sheikh

Duaij bin Ali was constantly moving and active, and he would never tire of dispelling the silence with exciting talk and disturbing the calm with small events.

Our sitting close to the beach would give me an opportunity to observe the features and actions of the passersby. The pedestrians from amongst the farmers and fishermen who would return home exhausted from the hard day's work and whose steps were rushed by urgent needs, who greeted us with salutations hurriedly, so much so that they would almost miss hearing a reply. Others would entertain us by slow greetings, enjoying our hospitality, and exchanging conversations with us.

As for the evening assembly, it took place in the big house in Muharraq, and it concurred—in the course of the conversations and their coordination—with the daytime gatherings, were it not for the fact that attendance would be increased by the attendance of a number of close friends, such as Sheikh Abdullah bin Khaled and Sheikh Omar, along with a group of Bedouins from the desert and a group of falcon hunters. Another additional guest was the falcon, that could not find an arm that was suitable for carrying it and did not like to perch except on its base in front of the owner assigned to it. Therefore, holes and more holes in the floor of the room multiplied with all those who attended after hunting in the spring season. And the falcon would not stop turning its head or flapping its wings, and it would spin around in a provocation and aggressiveness that elicited caution as much as it seized admiration and pride. The falcon would not stop and rest until pieces of meat were presented to him to consume or a skin cover was placed over his eyes.

That kind of situation prevailed for us for a year or more during the publication of *Al-Ansar* magazine until the "surprise" occurred.

Further, the discussion about that surprise actually includes three surprises instead of one: The first was that *Al-Ansar* magazine suddenly decided to cease publishing after the issue of Dhul-Hijjah of the year 1363 AH, and the second was that the magazine secretly revealed the truth of the identity of *Al-Ansar's* anonymous writers—that Muhammad Dhafer, Hamid Abu Al-Ataya, Sadeq Al-Hakim, and Hussam were only pseudonyms, and all the lengthy articles and research papers that have been published bearing these names came from Ahmed Sabry himself, the owner of *Al-Ansar*. Thus, Ahmed's writing and effort bore him the burden of editing the magazine and issuing it for four continuous years, in addition to the "messages" issued by *Al-Ansar*, with the exception of the relatively few articles in which real writers participated. One of the real writers in *Al-Ansar* was the Jordanian activist, Mr. Fahad Al-Rimawi.

The third surprise was that the owner of *Al-Ansar*, along with his colleagues—who have become like family members—who worked with him on *Al-Ansar*, had decided to migrate from the narrow world of cities to the vast expanse of the desert. Ahmed Sabry said, "The voice of Al-Ansar has spoken the truth, so that its voice might reach out to you amid hardship and scarcity of resources. And those who believe in these explicit rights for mankind will be saved, God willing." Then he added, "As for this issue, we made the conclusion of speaking glad tidings to our brothers and friends, and to our opponents as well!"

The readers of *Al-Ansar* magazine became upset at the news of its ceasing publication. Surprise, mixed with sorrow and bitterness, followed the *Al-Ansar* group and its supporters, as if they had not expected that this bold voice would be silenced and that those bright flashes would be cut off one day.

Then the confusion dissipated and the effect of the shock eased, so they were divided into two groups: a group that praised the experience and a group that showed affection, then held on at this point. Professor Hasan al-Jishi was at the forefront of these, as his presence in Cairo following the suspension of *Al-Ansar* magazine gave him the opportunity to get to know Ahmed Sabry personally. Through him, Professor Ibrahim Al-Arrayed contacted the owner of *Al-Ansar*, and he gifted him verses of honest and expressive poetry.

Ahmed Sabry replied to it in a letter in which he described the impact of these verses on him by saying,

"As for your poem, you set a distant goal for me with it. I still open my eyes and close my eyes to it."

Moreover, another team was excited about the new march and saw the possibility of a continuation with it. However, this great question remained, "What comes after the migration?" That question hung in the air without a definitive answer. And whenever the urgent question transgressed the immediate goal of migration—which was "purifying the soul"—to distant goals, the unknown future seemed shrouded in mystery.

Thus, Sheikh Khalid Al-Khalifa became interested in *Al-Ansar*'s idea of "migration." He, therefore, traveled after that to the tents of Bani Khalid—east of the Arabian Peninsula—and the rhymes of poetry struggled to bid him farewell with every incoming and outgoing. Then he returned after nearly six years, and we listened to him expressing his feelings of elation, and he considered those years a useful and indispensable experience in his life.

Among those who went out to the desert, among the Iraqi supporters of *Al-Ansar*, was the writer and poet Hilal Naji. So he journeyed to the outskirts of the desert, satirizing the life of the cities, saying:

"In the land of the civil dwellings, souls wither away and the crowds perish in descent and division."

Then he came back home after two or three years, and he said:

"I am sorry for the life I have lived, as I spent half of it in disappointment and half of it in the pursuit of hopes."

As for the head of *Al-Ansar*'s migration to the desert, Mr. Ahmad Sabry Shuwaiman, he left Cairo with his family to live amongst the tribes of the Sinai desert. After a few years of staying there, he found Sinai to be a difficult place for his family and decided to stay on the outskirts of the city of Port Said with the peasants in Alshallufa village. He changed his name from Ahmad Sabry to his family name: **"Ahmad Moosa Salem."**

He became a prominent imam in his village. That was during the era of the popular Egyptian President, Jamal Abdul Nasser.

Abdul Nasser formed a political party (the United Socialist Party) consisting of 25% from labor unions and 25% from the peasants. Forming, with other supporters, the majority in the Parliament. In a new cession of the parliament, the village where Ahmed Salem lived was asked to nominate a member to the Parliament, and they voted to nominate Ahmed Salem, who joined the Parliament thereafter.

During his Parliamentary representation, he was chosen, along with others, for a diplomatic mission to Europe and the Middle East, which gave him the opportunity to promote his ideas regarding Islam. He wrote a book about those meetings and arguments with the West called, "Forming Family Affairs in the Light of Islam."

He retired from the Parliament after that and settled in a simple flat in Halwan, on the outskirts of Cairo. I paid him a visit in 1973. I offered him money to help needy families, but he refused instantly with suspicion.

Ahmed Moosa finished his above-mentioned book in 1994. After his death, I printed his book in 1996. The Syrian press refused to print the book—perhaps because he had criticized some of the Syrian ministers in the book. So I printed the book in Lebanon.

The introduction to his book was written by: 1) Dr. Alsayed Risq Al-Tawil, former Dean of the faculty of Arabic and Islamic studies at Al-Azhar University, member of the High Committee for Islamic Affairs, and Chief President of Al-Haqq Islamic Societies; and 2) by his friend, Abdul Ghani Said. Both writers admitted that Moosa Salem was a genius thinker and reformist.

Dr. Rizq mentioned what Sheikh Ahmed Hassan Albaqouri (one of the Chief Presidents of Al-Azhar University) said about Moosa Salem, quote, "This man is like Prophet Ibrahim Al-Khalil; he was the Abraham of his era."

Nonetheless, *Al-Ansar* became a crucial part of my childhood memories as well as those of later years, even so as to affect me deeply now.

*

NOTE: I included more details about *Al-Ansar* in my book, "Colored Papers." I estimate that my research is the first, or perhaps the most unique, to authenticate *Al-Ansar* from an insider's point of view.

**

= 9 =
Baghdad: Dar As-Salam (the House of Peace)

*

Our meeting in Dar As-Salaam, Baghdad,
And how many memories she has in my heart,
The Tigris River gave her beauty and attraction,
And the bouquets of palm trees, high in the sky,
Their roots, delved deep into the depths of the soil,
Gardens provided lovers with a refreshing breeze and sweet perfume,
And the full moon broke the darkness, pathways to glamorous dawn,
Peaks of ancestral glories throughout history, made by those who built them with firm determination,
Against invaders, from the East and the West.

*

Studying in Iraq has a very interesting place in my memory. The aforementioned verses of poetry that I composed in the eighties come close to being able to explain the deepness of my love for Iraq.

The English Director of Education in Bahrain in 1943, who was from the British Council Institute and who succeeded Mr. Wakelin, had suddenly decided to nominate a group of students to complete their studies in Egypt. My brother Hussein and I were at the top of the list of candidates for it. I remember that I carried the news to my father with joy, but then a wall of deep silence built up between us, then he finally broke his silence, saying, "I do not agree. The world has become dark in my eyes." Despite the efforts of my older brother, Sadiq, to incite the mediators who had an influence on him, my father—may God have mercy on him—insisted on his rejectionist position under the pretext of fearing for our religion and morals, considering Cairo as a place for singing and dancing and low moral standards.

One day after I greeted him in the morning while I was about to kiss his hand, he smiled cheerfully then said, "I have read in some of the interpretations in the explanation of the Holy Qur'an the Almighty's saying: 'And do not kill your children for fear of poverty.' That depriving children of seeking knowledge is a kind of killing of their souls that God does not accept." For this reason, he agreed to allow me to travel with my brother Hussein to study abroad—not to Egypt but to Iraq—at his expense instead of the government's because Iraq was closer than Egypt and there were relatives and family friends there who would take care of us.

My brother Sadiq was overjoyed, and he resolved our hesitation in volunteering to carry out the role of the guardian. And our older brother, thankfully, fulfilled with the role with which he was entrusted. At the height of his preoccupation with completing travel formalities, he did not forget to direct us to get a letter of recommendation from the Ministry of Education. So, I went with my brother Hussein to greet the late Sheikh Abdullah bin Isa Al-Khalifa (Head of Education) at his council in the Muharraq Municipality Building. Thanks to the help and attention of the kind gentleman, Mr. Ibrahim Hassan Kamal, we received the long-awaited letter in a short period of time. Then we traveled, putting our trust in God. That was in the year 1944.

We arrived in Baghdad, and the school year had already begun. Then we went to the Ministry of Education to meet with its Minister at the time, Mahmoud Al-Alusi, and in its courtyard began the first confrontation between us and the meticulous routine enrollment procedures. We were required to first start with writing a petition to the Ministry of Education by finding one of the writers of petitions, who sat outside the front entrance of the Ministry, waiting with their small writing box to prepare an enroller's petition according to the style inherited from the Turkish era. It took a few days to record and number it, after which Sadiq began the task of transferring the petition and its various attachments between multiple offices and halls, and he had to hustle with the auditors and appease the doormen to have the opportunity to appear before the competent official, after hours of training in the face of the question and answer, and to gather courage in the face of the one who was in control of the situation, the official, who was often satisfied with taking a quick look at the petition and then pointing at it and throwing it to the gatekeeper at best, or moving it aside, repeating the familiar phrase, "Come back tomorrow." Because of the nature of this process, we found ourselves having passed the middle of the second month of the school year while we still did not know the fate of our admission.

Our saving grace came to us in the help of Professor Salman Al-Safwani. He was familiar with the Minister, had a leadership position in the Istiqlal Party, and published the well-known newspaper, *Al-Yaqthah*. He was also a friend of my father.

Thankfully, Professor Al-Safwani accomplished the commendable endeavor, and His Excellency the Minister asked for the papers of the petition and began to turn them over with emotion, as he was astonished at the subjection of the transactions of Gulf Arab students to these long procedures while they are guests of Iraq. Since the whole issue was about admission to the school and hostel accommodation, the Minister spoke by phone to the director of the secondary school and the director of the boarding department, and the problem was resolved on the spot. We went to meet the director of Al-Adhamiya High School, and he welcomed us, and at last we felt the warmth of passion that characterized the authentic Iraqi people. Thus, it was upon us to decide whether to enroll in the scientific or literary section classes, and a quick look at the scientific curriculum was enough to divert us from it and persuade us to choose the literary section. The science material we had learned in Bahrain had been far below the required standard. On the contrary, our literary level in Arabic and English studies was much higher, to the extent that I was exempted, according to the system in final examinations, from submitting the final exam, with the exception of mathematics and the biographic history of Iraq. Another classmate with us from Bahrain was of Bahrain royal family descent (Sheikh Duaij bin Ali Al-Khalifa). He faced the same difficulties of the routine system of enrollment at the Ministry but was assisted by our arrangement with the Minister and joined us later.

The Iraqi students welcomed our presence with them, and a number of them developed bonds of fellowship and friendship with us. We had reservations about them leaving the classroom for political reasons. It was common for one of them to stand by surprise and clap his hands, announcing, "Everybody must leave school at once! There's a demonstration taking place!" Students would follow him and leave the school during recess and sometimes even in the middle of their lessons, so the teachers got into the habit of collecting their papers hurriedly as they would flee the classroom with haste.

The three of us Bahrainis would stay in class, as we felt that we were outsiders. But the kind high school principal advised us after that to go out with the others to avoid their indignation. So, we did, but instead of attending the demonstrations, we would return to our hostel.

The patriotic sentiments in Iraq were at their highest in the second half of the 1940s, especially with the spreading news of negotiations with Britain to end the Iraqi treaty and conclude a new one under the new name of the "Portsmouth Treaty."

We used to listen to the news of the loud demonstrations and read about them on the front pages of the daily newspapers, and I was very impressed by the enthusiastic poems that were published from time to time, especially the poems of Muhammad Salih Bahr al-Ulum, for whom I attended one of the celebrations in the courtyard of Holy Mashhad al-Kadhimiya when he had just been released from prison. He directed his speech, pointing with his hand to where Abd Ul-Ilah (Guardian of King Faisal) and Nuri Al-Saeed (Prime Minister) were sitting in the VIP lounge, saying: "These are the palaces of the traitors, surrounded by innocents who are threatened by gallows and graves." It was said that after this celebration, he was arrested and sent back to prison! I also admired the poet Muhammad Mahdi Al-Jawahiri.

At that time, the parties and newspapers, speaking on their platforms, competed in bidding to win the masses and arouse their patriotic feelings—at a time when they were seeking political gains toward the government or toward other parties. At the forefront of those parties were the Independence Party and its leader Mahdi Kubba, its Secretary General Faeq al-Samarrai, and its newspaper, *Istiqlal*. As for the Secretary of the Independence Party, he was Professor Salman al-Safwani, and his newspaper was *Al-Yaqdhah*. There was also the National Democratic Party and its head, Kamel Chadirji, and its newspaper, *Al-Ahali*. Then there was the Liberal Party, as well, in favor of Saleh Jabr and its newspaper, *Al-Zaman*—supposedly the hero of the ill-fated Treaty of Portsmouth, but it was known that its true hero was Nuri Al-Saeed. Then there was the secret Communist Party and other small parties. The Ba'ath Party was founded in 1947. At that time, it did not have an audible voice. As a result of the public's general negative attitude against Britain, the accusation of collaborating with the English became commonplace. And we came to expect from the Iraqi friends we got to know better—after the words of welcome and praise for the Arabism of Bahrain had ended—that this question would always be asked: "What are you going to do about the British Occupation?"

One of the funniest memories that I recollect about Nuri Al-Saeed is when he ordered the allocation of a school in the name of "the College of Science," located opposite to the hostel in which we used to live. This college was chosen to teach English, along with English cultural customs and manners, to students who would be nominated to complete their studies in Britain. They were wearing special uniforms similar to those of English university students. These "luxury" students were subjected to the wrath and ridicule of the Iraqi students, as they gathered around them upon their entry and exit and called them the "tails of the colonizers." From the time of the Turks, Kadhimiya and Adhamiya were connected across the river by a swinging wooden bridge. One day, a large herd of giant buffaloes passed over the bridge, and then they broke free and ran off, inciting fear in onlookers, and their crazed stampede did not stop except at the location of that unfortunate college, so its wire fence was demolished and the trees and plants in its garden were mowed down. The crowd said, "Even Iraqi buffaloes hate colonialism!"

In the midst of this charged political atmosphere, the royal palace was trying hard to keep people's thoughts busy with news of royal honors, visits, parties, and celebrations, and the establishment of wedding and mourning seasons. Then the royal wedding season arrived, and the famous songstress Umm Kulthum attended, and Iraqis flocked to Baghdad, decorations and joy parties spread, and a block of streets was laid out with carpets. Baghdad stayed up all night until the morning, listening to the voice of Umm Kulthum.

*

At the Students' Hostel Accommodation

We lived in the Arab scholarship missions' hall, which was a large rectangular hall that could accommodate over twenty beds. My brother Hussein and I were located in some of the first sleeping beds, and we had a third student from the Hijaz named Hussein al-Dabbagh next to us. To our left extended the students on scholarships from southern Arabia, Indonesia, and Java, most of whom were of Arab origin. As for the other beds, they were inhabited by the Arab students from Syria and Al-Iskandarona (a Syrian district occupied by the Turkish authorities), which was referred to by the Syrians as the "Stolen Land." As for the leader of the Javanese students, his name was Abu Bakr. As for the leader of the other side, his name was Mr. Fayez Ismail, who later became the Minister of State in Syria. Both leaders were united in two advantages: the first was their diligence in lessons and revision, and the second was that each of them was distinguished by his attractive personality, great manners, witty sense of humor, and lighthearted spirit. But other than those common qualities, they differed in everything under the sun! Our position between these two groups had become like a material barrier. I always wondered about this phenomenon whenever I found that the two groups lived together in one hall while simultaneously each was living in their own world. At that time, I understood the nature of human relationships, especially the human soul, whereby the psychological and cultural barriers could form a wall of isolation thicker than a wall, by choice and decision.

Abu Bakr was fond of music and dance and invited his companions to participate in them.

He used to wake up at 5:30 in the morning and dance alone or with his companions to Latin American music and songs from among his phonograph record disks.

Fayez Ismail used to spend his spare time studying. When he was not focusing on his studies, he used to hold discussions with his followers in peace and quiet. I saw Professor Michel Aflaq (head of the Ba'ath Party) participate in those meetings. They would sometimes take place in the quiet corner of the lobby of our hostel hall, which witnessed the beginning of the birth of the Iraqi Ba'ath Party a few years before its official announcement.

Our relationship with everyone we met was one of friendship and mutual respect. Although I was not comfortable with dancing, I did enjoy the melody of those delicate Spanish tunes. I came across them a lot after that, and it reminded me—and still reminds me every time I hear it—of those days. On the other hand, the idea of *Al-Ansar* distracted me from the ideas of the Arab Ba'ath Party, and Fayez Ismail understood this, so we avoided holding frequent discussions.

*

Adhamiya town was a beautiful and quiet residential area that combined city life and the beauty of the countryside. In addition, it contained the grave of Imam Abu Hanifa and his shrine on one side, along with the royal cemetery with its exquisite architecture on the other side of the river, near the inner part. When I used to walk to school in the morning, I would avoid the traffic and crowded paved street, take a short cut through farms and palm groves, and on either side of the winding, dusty road I would find two contrasting phenomena: to my left were the luxury residences with their beautiful gardens, where roses and flowers abounded, and orange trees hung behind their walls. On the right side, there were tall palm groves interspersed with small housing complexes for farmers and their families. They were brown mud huts in the depression that followed the embankment of the river, so they were exposed, before others, to the dangers of floods. And you would find these mud huts very small and low-ceilinged, as if they had been built for dwarves, and you could watch from a distance the heads of the people who lived in them. Thus, if you were taken aback by curiosity enough to approach them, being indifferent to the provocation of the barking dogs, you could watch most of what was going on inside of the rural household as if you were watching the open theater.

We shared with other Iraqi students their life in the hostel, with its bitterness and its sweetness. On happy occasions, cooking was good, and dishes were filled with delicious food. But in the absence of the watchdog, as the quality and quantity of food would decrease, there would be widespread discontent, and students would strike for food. The strike would begin, and those in charge would throw huge quantities of food in the sewers or in the dumpsters outside—hills of rice, meat, vegetables, and butter would be wasted.

On days like these when there was a hunger strike, I used to go out with Sheikh Duaij bin Ali—as we always did—to the Rusafa Cafe along the Tigris River, and we waited in the usual corner, then Lawyer Khaled Al-Aldayi (from the *Al-Ansar* Iraqi group) would join us, along with a group of friends. As for Hilal Naji (Head of *Al-Ansar* in Iraq), he would join the gathering later on, after he took off his English uniform and put on the traditional clothing of the Iraqi tribesmen. We would be busy during these sessions with the talk of *Al-Ansar* and the news received from Bahrain about Sheikh Khalid bin Muhammad, who had migrated to live amongst desert tribes in Eastern Saudi Arabia, poems by Abdulaziz Al-Qadi, and general news. Then Hilal would recite some of his poetry. He would stare at us at the end of the passage, as if to say, "Why don't you say, 'Well done.'" So we would say it and ask for more. When the assembly ended, he would insist on offering us a meal. He would not calm down unless we agreed with him to walk to his nearby house or accompany him—oftentimes—to a place on the side of the entrance from Al-Rasheed Street, where it led us to a well-known "dairy house" shop that offered us dates, milk, yogurt, and its derivatives. That was the ideal food that the people of *Al-Ansar* would describe as the "perfect" food.

= 10 =
From School Desk to Business Desk

*

What kept me from continuing my university studies was my reluctance to take up career positions, so I turned to practicing commerce since the end of 1946, when I was on the verge of 17 years of age. I chose instead self-education by reading my brother Hussein's books when he was studying at the Law College in Baghdad, in addition to a wide range of educational and knowledge books.

My duty was to help my father in his commercial business and to learn from him, as he was working in the import and export trade and selling goods from outside Bahrain on a commission of 3% in the field of dry foods and food supplies, as well as other consumable commodities. The sea route was the main source for import and export and for travel as well, Bahrain being an island. As for the means of transportation, they were the large sailing ships, known by distinct names, and they used to roam the seas between Africa and the coasts of India and the Gulf. As for hand-crafted boats with engines (launches), they were—due to their small size— mostly confined to moving between the coasts of the Gulf countries.

The other main means of transporting goods and passengers were commercial ships, most of which operated between India and the Gulf, a few of them reaching Bahrain directly from remote international ports. For this reason, most of those goods came into Bahrain via India on Indian ships, which were called, according to their destination, *"Al-Ma'ali"* (if ships heading from India to Basra of Iraq) and *"Sannan"* if they were returning to India. At that time, the most important concern of merchants and travelers was the arrival time of *Al-Ma'ali* and *Sannan*, and many people would rush to the coast of the sea port to check for the arrival of the boat by sighting it in the distance. Due to the small seaport of Manama, the big ships used to anchor far away, at a distance of not less than four miles from Manama.

My father owned a number of hand-crafted ships and used them to transport goods that belonged to him or that were sent to him. On a number of occasions, I had been present when he heard the news of the sinking of a ship with its goods belonging to him, so he used to keep calm and did not complain aloud but would just talk to the captain of the sunken vessel in a quiet tone. He would ask him first about the safety of the crews and say, "If souls were saved, money doesn't matter." He, may Allah have mercy on him, was impressed by the chant of this line of poetry: "If human souls are saved, money is subject to risk."

When the native ships arrived at the port, the captain would descend from them with a retinue in line behind him and the sailors following closely behind in their modest Omani attire, wearing turbans and colorful clothing, and in each hand they held a long bamboo stick. As for the captains of the Gulf and their sailors, their clothes were simple, and they would carry in their hands rosary beads instead of sticks.

As soon as the simple procedures for clearing goods from the port and customs were completed, the contractors would transport them to the warehouses on donkeys or in small carts, each pulled by a big donkey! In the past, donkeys in Bahrain were famous for their strength, beauty, and whiteness. They were once among the most desirable commodities in neighboring countries, and their owners would export them abroad after fulfilling the required specifications and obtaining a special permit to transport them out of the country.

Moreover, if we imagine that the cargo that had just arrived at the port consisted of a thousand or two thousand bags, then what followed this conception would undoubtedly be the scene of a long caravan of these large, white donkeys dyed with reddish henna on their legs, walking at a medium pace, between jogging and running, each carrying two or three bags on his back. Each of those donkeys was dressed in a small hanging bell, which served to warn the unaware of its path on the road. They must be hit with sticks on their backs to urge them to walk or on one side of the neck to change the direction of the advance to the direction of the market and its narrow, dusty roads.

The contractors had great skill in handling and lifting the bags—which weighed 56 pounds each—from the ground on their own, then tightening them to one side of the donkey with half a tie of rope, from which the rest would hang in order to receive a second bag on the other side; then they would even add a third one on top of the other two bags on the unfortunate donkeys. All of that took place while the patient donkey opened its long ears, and the pupils of its eyes focused on the stick so that it would not miss any of the instructions of its owner, who spoke loudly with specific sounds recognized by the donkey, along with some signals and commands accompanied by the threat of using the stick, so the donkey would understand what was meant by that and stand still or move accordingly, while the movements of its tail indicated its boredom from waiting or its muffled anxiety. Then it would move at the whim of its driver and lean with him to the left and right, wherever he wished. Nonetheless, nothing would disturb the donkey's owner more than the donkey stopping to exercise some of its natural rights or its freedom to stand and test its voice by braying. And if he was deprived of that and there was a blatant protest against the heavy load, he would stop with it, reluctant to continue walking, and would not be deterred by a beating or reprimand.

Donkeys were also used after working hours.

I remember one day that one of the foreigners asked me jokingly—as he had seen a caravan of donkeys wading in the sea that evening to transport fish from the fisheries—whether the donkey also worked overtime in the afternoon or if they were considered an amphibious means of transportation…

*

Among the other skills that I learned at my father's shop were the principles of buying and selling and that the majority of wholesale sale deals were facilitated through brokers. In order to preserve business secrets from other visitors while in an open office, brokers would be obliged to whisper in my father's ear the details of buying or selling. If an agreement was reached, my father would insist on recording the details of the transaction in a journal and would ask the broker to sign it on behalf of the party whom he represented.

Most small merchants did not adhere to my father's method of writing and signing the minutes of sales and, rather, preferred to pay an amount in advance—a deposit—pending the receipt of the goods. My father insisted on signing but would accept the deposit reluctantly. My father's religious obligation did not allow him to confiscate the deposit unrightfully in the case of the buyer retracting!

On Saturdays, I was obliged to collect the weekly outstanding debts of my father's clients. Payments were accepted in Indian silver rupees. In my father's office, I would have to count the money coins (silver Indian rupees) again and test their quality by throwing them at a smooth, hard stone and excluding the bad ones according to the sound of the ringing.

Another job that I was tasked with was making copies of outgoing letters and invoices. I would use an old "press" on the copybook by means of a damp cloth, as well as translating letters and telegrams from and into English. One of the strenuous experiences was weighing the rice or wheat bags with a weighing scale, each of them weighing in at around 55 lbs. This slow process took place near warehouses, at the terminal, or on the deck of the ship at sea, without regard to the arduous working conditions or the times of rest and food. The important thing was to receive or deliver as quickly as possible! I had to use a "tally" book to record the weight of each bag with the time and hour of shipment and write my signature on the total number of bags and the total weight of all the bags combined.

Father: Blessing and Encouragement

At the end of 1947, I decided to travel to Pakistan and India, and they were in their first era of partition.

On the ship to Karachi, there were a number of small merchants from Kuwait, Bahrain, and Dubai, most of whom were called "gold merchant smugglers."

Soon after, the news appeared in the newspapers about the disgraceful behavior of gold smugglers, while I myself understood the secret of the crowding between them over the toilets on the ship before it reached the port.

My father, may Allah have mercy on him, gave me two recommendations: The first was directed to the notable merchant from Kuwait, Saud Abdul-Aziz Al-Fulaij, when I visited him in his office in Karachi, which included his Majlis and his residence. So, I agreed to accept his request to eat lunch with him daily, and I did not regret that, as the food was delicious. And I would go to visit him in the evenings to listen to the radio, especially the news of the Palestinian war and the partition proposal of Palestine by the assembly of the United Nations in 1948. He would turn the volume of the radio down as low as possible, which reminded me of the days of the Second World War and Berlin's banned radio station in Bahrain.

The second letter from my father I carried to the Pakistani merchant, Hajj Geeta Bai Gokul, and his office in Karachi on the upper floor of a building in the old market in the middle of a narrow road. Then Hajj Geeta received me with respect and hospitality, with his receding hairline and fragile body, as he received a merchant from his regular clients. A large table was filled with a group of his friends and business acquaintances. Overnight, I became a guest of honor at the table of a rich and famous man who owns a fleet of ships of about 138 or more. I compared this reception, which brought me great confidence and confirmed a sense of responsibility at a stage in my life of self-affirmation, along with the interview with Dr. Balushi, the renowned doctor who had a medicine clinic in Bahrain and, in turn, was a close friend of my father and our family physician. But he treated me as if I was still that little boy in his eyes.

From Karachi, I decided to travel to Bombay, and I was astonished on the day of travel when I found that all ships and means of transportation had become harnessed for the exchange of population migration between India and Pakistan. I would have decided to postpone my trip had it not been for a group of Omani sailors passing by who recognized me and said, "This is the son of our master, Haji Muhammad Albaharna." Then they carried me on their shoulders with my luggage and made a place for me on the deck of the ship among those crowds of Hindus. Then they set up my folded bed among them, and whenever I raised my head a little, I saw around me a sea of Hindu heads and Sikh turbans, and I had no need to visit Bombay except for my curiosity, getting to know my father's friends, and observing the markets. And it was also well known at the time that its water and air were polluted, unlike those of Karachi.

I was a guest of the Eminent Haji Jaafar Abdul Rahim in his house, and with him there were his family business friends Haji Ahmed, Haji Haider Darwish, and Haji Ibrahim Mahmoud; all of them were famous Gulf merchants. Cows were roaming, pedestrians crowded on the sidewalks, and traffic was disrupted at the signals without anyone protesting. I also saw, at the height of the crowdedness, people whose bodies were stained with mud and dyes walking naked. After that, I realized that they were men of the temples, and I witnessed the spread of poverty and the use of sidewalks for living and sleeping. However, the most important thing that stuck in my mind, from a commercial point of view, was my attendance for the first time in my life at an industrial and commercial exhibition, and I was astonished by the development of industry in India. One of the best parts was that the exhibitors celebrated me and exchanged cards and addresses with me as if I were a well-known merchant!

The journey back from Bombay to Karachi was a far cry from my journey to Bombay. My father, after knowing the kind of hardship I suffered traveling on the deck of the ship, wrote to Haji Jaffar Abdul Rahim, insisting that I return to Karachi with a first-class ticket, irrespective of the cost. I got a place in the first class and enjoyed its privileges and amenities. However, hundreds of Pakistanis, who were returning from Bombay to Karachi, were staring at me from behind the stained glass and focusing their looks and gestures toward me, excluding other first-class travelers. A well-dressed lady, who appeared to have features of wealth, and a number of escorting maids in tow, as well as two English gentlemen, who addressed her as "Begum," invited me to sit at her table. And I cannot remember, from our many conversations and stories, anything about her except that she owns factories and farms and that she knows the leader Gandhi very well and knows a great deal about his private life. Further, I also met a rich Englishman who owned sugar factories in Pakistan. I liked the exchange of knowledge with all of these people, as they were addressing me as if I were actually a businessman and not a young man in the first era of commerce. This reminded me of what was mentioned in one of my father's letters of advice, in which he wrote, "…Your reference to the occurrence of cholera in the country is not true—thank Allah that the country is pure. Do not limit yourself, and be in comfort and rest.

Further, you must behave with the best manners and be moderate with the merchants. Thus, you will be appreciated by them. And don't forget to tell me which of them are the best in their manners with you."

I asked Begum why the crowd outside was singling me out with their stares and what they were saying. She said that they were saying that you were wearing Arab attire, which means that you are wealthy and you are a Muslim in faith, so they hope you will be kind to them. They are Muslim immigrants and need help. Then she advised me to wear English clothing so that I would not be recognized. I did not find anything in my suitcase except a khaki scout's school uniform with shorts instead of trousers, but I thereby saved myself from intrusiveness.

I arrived in Karachi, put my Arab clothing back on, and got off the ship. When I arrived at the entrance to the building, a Pakistani stopped me and started looking at my clothes, asking permission to touch them. He asked me if these were the clothes of the Arabs since the time of the Prophet, upon whom be peace, and his Companions. I hesitated to answer and was afraid that the love of seeking blessings would lead him to ask me to give it to him to attain its blessings. If he had taken it from me, I would have been forced to return to Bahrain wearing a scout suit! However, when I was alone with myself afterward, I felt the extent of how disgraceful it is for an Arab to misbehave this way in a Muslim country while he is wearing the apparel of the Arabs, which they believe is the apparel of the Greatest Messenger (peace be upon him) and his Companions and that they would be blessed by it!

I returned to Bahrain in early 1948 and learned more about the news of the popular demonstrations on the occasion of the partition of Palestine, and I received some news of them in Karachi. These events, which I did not witness myself and which lasted for three continuous days and in which various groups of people participated in support of the struggle of the Palestinian Arab people, were considered the largest popular gathering of their kind during the years of the first half of this century. It was clear that those demonstrations were not destined to lead to the violence and attacks that coincided with them on the third day, until after that the Chancellor Charles Belgrave came to reveal in his book the reality of his experience with those incidents, mainly attacking Jews in their homes and stealing their belongings, that the aforementioned attacks were carried out by mobs of the sailors of the anchored ships in the port and not by residents of their neighborhood in Manama, while the good citizens had done what honesty and chivalry required of them.

*

Soon thereafter, I decided to travel to Iraq during the Palestinian war. I was, like many others, eager to liberate the land of Palestine, hoping for the Arab armies to carry out the task. I was a naïve, unexperienced boy, so I took a Palestinian map and marked the positions of Arab armies who were stationed in Palestine basecamps, put a date, as well as question mark, and an empty place to add the date of the completion of its liberation. Then I hung it on the wall over my bed. I waited for a long time, but when I heard that the Iraqi army—along with the other Arab armies—did not make any move, saying "*Maku Awamer*," i.e., "We have no order to attack," I remembered what had happened yesterday in Baghdad, when the Iraqi army was parading in the streets of Baghdad in a parade march on its way to Palestine (as they said), and the crowds threw roses and chanted loudly, "Make (Tel) Aviv, (WADY) of Aviv!" (TELL) in Arabic means Hill. And (WADY) means Valley) i.e., the crowd chanting encourages the Iraqi army to destroy Telavi in Palestine!! So, in my anguish and heartbreak, I took the map down from my wall and tore it to shreds.

*

My brother Sadiq and I, with the encouragement of our father, facilitated several business deals on our own. When he was convinced of our ability to work independently, he gave each of us ten thousand rupees, and we opened, in our own names, a shop under the name, "The Capital Store," for import, export, and commission. At that time, Europe, America, Japan, and Australia were the main sources of luxury and electrical goods, canned foods, fruit drinks, and other goods that the consumer public had been waiting for because of their lack of markets during the years of the war. The customers used to accept these commodities with a greedy sense of consumerism, and they would buy everything that they could get their hands on, especially if it was one of the products available to buy using the government family ration card, even if it was something of which they were not particularly in need.

The government would monitor prices, and the merchant would profit because of the volume of sales and the low costs; as for consumers, they were satisfied with what were able to get of imported goods!

Moreover, there would periodically be new faces to appear in the business arena who had left their regular jobs and ventured into practicing this unconventional type of trade. It was an opportunity to emerge and grow naturally and gradually. Furthermore, such middle-class merchants put forth much effort to raise their chances of success through their own hard work, and they would knock on the doors of wealth that had been welded shut. They were not among the wealthy of war, those who manipulated ration cards, or from those oil-rich fortunate persons.

Trade Is the Graveyard of Talents

During my work in trade, my connection with the *Al-Ansar* family was not severed, neither with men of thought, literature, nor the activities of cultural clubs. A group of writers and poets would frequently gather in our shop, headed by our great professor Ibrahim Al-Arrayed, who used to visit us daily most of the time, along with Ali Altajir, Hassan Al-Jishi, Duaij Al-Khalifa, and Abdullah Al-Tai, and writers from the Kingdom in Qatif, Al-Khobar, and Al-Ahsa, including Ahmed Al-Rashed Al-Mubarak, Abdul-Aziz Al-Qadi, Muhammad Saeed Al-Muslim, Abd Al-Rasoul Al-Sheikh, Ali Al-Jishi, Ahmad Al-Mustafa, and others.

I used to go out with some of them for an evening walk outside the city then rest in some popular café, and I remember that Mr. Ali Altajir kept carrying under his arm every time we met a huge book in English, the book "My Struggle" by Hitler—given that he was studying it on the basis of his research on Zionism—until the copy of the book was worn out and torn in places. He always assured us, biting his lips nervously and in a defiant manner, that the Jews were the source of all evil in the world and that behind every phenomenon that seemed strange and mysterious to people, Jewish hands were controlling it and distributing its roles on the stage of the world with malice and cunning. Further, that idea commenced with the secrets of global policies, Zionist forums, and conspiracies against peoples and governments. And because he was skilled in persuasion and effective at arguing, I used to take many of his opinions seriously and compliment him on others, but either way, I did not take them for granted.

Mr. Maan Al-Ijly was an Iraqi friend. When he got tired of arguing with Mr. Altajir, he used to leave our office instantly, saying to me, "Oh, my brother, business does not suit you. Leave commerce and go into literature and writing as an intellectual thinker. Have I not told you many times before that commerce is a graveyard of talents?"

Our shop was also on the way to and from the Government of Bahrain Judicial Court. The well-known head of justice for religious affairs, Sheikh Abdul Husain Al-Hilli, used to take his breaks in our shop on his way to and from the Judicial Court. He was also a great poet and a recognized writer. I used to discuss with him religious matters as well as poetry. Our moral outcome from these visits of his to our shop was very useful and bright, even though the material outcome of sales was zero.

As for our gatherings with friends in our shop, my brother Sadiq—and sometimes my brother Hussein—and I would receive visits from a number of professors, university graduates, and young scholars each Friday.

*

Voice of Bahrain Magazine

Issuing a cultural magazine was always a dream in the back of the minds of the Board of Directors of the Orouba Club, which I mentioned in the previous chapter.

Most, if not all, of those names I mentioned above that used to hang out at our shop contributed to writing in the *Voice of Bahrain* magazine, which was issued in late 1949. Plus, if we add the names of other authors, poets, and writers in Bahrain, such as Mahmoud Al-Mardi, Ali Sayyar, Ibrahim Hassan Kamal, Muhammad Dwiger, Ahmed Yateem, Abdul Aziz Al-Shamlan, Youssef Zubari, Abdul Rahman Al-Maawdah, Abdul Aziz Sheikh Ali, Ahmed Salman Kamal, Nasser Buhumaid, Ahmed Al-Khalifa, and many others, we will realize the extent of the literary base that launched the Voice of Bahrain. It has attracted the finest talents and literary potential available, working to create a pioneering magazine in the history of Gulf journalism as a whole. Arab writers, originating from several Arab countries, have also contributed to the *Voice of Bahrain*. This magazine has become the shining face of culture, thought, and literature for Bahrain and the Gulf throughout the great Arab world.

The *Voice of Bahrain* addressed the concerns of the Arab citizen with honesty, sincerity, seriousness, and commitment. Its publication came years after the cessation of *Al-Ansar* magazine and after its echoes subsided, but the spirit and style of *Al-Ansar* magazine had a profound impact on the direction of the magazine with regard to awareness and cultural and intellectual guidance. It had a distinctive Arab national and Islamic characteristic and a frank style of delivery.

One of the most important things the *Voice of Bahrain* has devoted its efforts to—after cultural guidance—was dealing with social reform, fairness to the working population, and the adoption of workers' rights. On the other hand, the magazine defended Bahrain's Arab identity and refuted foreign claims of sovereignty over it. In this regard, the magazine translated and published a pamphlet by Professor Majid Khadduri on "Bahrain and Iran," and the magazine printed his book with a comprehensive presentation of each chapter. The great demand for purchasing the book led to his reprinting it for a second time. And it was no great surprise that the demand for the magazine itself was tremendous.

The magazine was eventually shut down for political and financial reasons around early 1952. In my opinion, the gap in the cultural and literary void left by the *Voice of Bahrain* still exists, even after nearly 37 years have passed, during which Bahrain has witnessed a leap in the field of education and has added university majors in the fields of literature, culture, science, and the arts.

It is worth noting that the greatest burden in editing and publishing the *Voice of Bahrain*—despite the existence of an editorial group as well as a board of directors—rested on Professor Hassan Jawad Al-Jishi, and then Ibrahim Hassan Kamal, and on the efforts of Ali Altajir. As for my role in the magazine, it was no more than writing a number of articles and filling the void in some sections when the magazine was ready for printing, then contributing to its distribution and filling it with some advertisements.

Our shop customers used to buy the magazine, which would be set out next to other commodities, such as electric fans, canned foods, cordial orange juice in the summertime, readymade garments, and sweets in the winter months.

People would rush to buy the magazine before it sold out.

Finally, the End of Memories

*

At this point, as we approach the fifties, we stand with these memories in their last episode. The fifties and their aftermath witnessed huge events in the history of Bahrain and various indications of all the political, cultural, economic, social, and psychological factors that have flowed through the veins of society since the beginning of the twentieth century in the form of small forked tributaries that poured all their momentum into a large reservoir in which the torrent streams gathered then filled and almost flooded. Waiting for the faithful, aware, and honest hands to direct the flowing water toward the thirsty land in order to produce security, fertility, and prosperity.

The era of the developments that took place in the fifties and beyond is not very far away, and, therefore, this stage of development to keep pace with the advanced march of the modern world is worthy to be a subject for study using the tools of history and the evidence of memoirs. Thus, it does not fall within the scope of these fleeting personal memories of a young boy.

Soon after the *Voice of Bahrain* magazine ceased publication, Bahrain witnessed in 1953 a political and social public uprising.

Hence, a "High Executive Committee" was formed in order to present demands for reform actions to His Highness Sheikh Salman bin Hamad Al-Khalifa, ruler of Bahrain, and Government Adviser Mr. William Belegrave. The committee took serious steps toward fulfilling working class demands to have a just labor laws. Thus, the "People's Committee" was formed for the first time in Bahrain and the Gulf states—the "Bahrain Labor Federation," which was founded without the consent of the government, to cooperate in establishing a new labor law and to discuss it with a committee formed by the government with the help of a labor adviser from Britain, namely Mr. Marshal, who was a member of the British Labor Committee. I was chosen to become the General Executive Secretary of the Bahrain Labor Federation. The High Executive Committee was recognized by the Bahrain Government in 1955 under the name of "Alwifaq Al Watany" as a licensed political party that had the capacity to negotiate public demands with the permission of the ruler of Bahrain and his adviser. The Government of Bahrain issued a decree permitting every 20 citizens to form a political party to discuss demands for political and social reforms. It is to be noted that no other Gulf countries in the Arabian Gulf had governmental permission to form political parties at that time.

The Alwifaq party was dissolved by the government in 1956 because of huge public demonstrations, which took place in support of Egypt after the invasion by Britain, France, and Israel during the Suez Canal War. Another reason was, perhaps, that in the same year, British Foreign Minister Mr. Selwyn Lloyd arrived in Bahrain and was subject to stones being thrown at his car, as well as people following him and trying to escort him back out of the country.

Mr. Belgrave formed a Court of Security Justice, which issued a court decision to send three of the men of the Alwifaq party to be imprisoned on the island of Saint Helena and the rest to the Bahrain Prison, with the exception of the head of the movement, Sayed Ali Kamal Uddin, who chose to leave Bahrain and stay in Iraq.

**

THE END

With my brother, Husain

With my father

My photo in the secondary school period

My photo during study period in Iraq

My photos in our shop

Glass Marbles

Spinning top

With my brother, Sadiq, and Mr. Jassim Albaqer

With Mr. Helal Naji in Baghdad

With my friends

With Nadi al-Orouba members on a trip

My teacher, Abdulrasool Al Tajer

My teacher, Abdulrasool Al Tajer, with his students

Bahraini kids studying Quran in Katateeb

The opening of Jafaria School

Manama Market in the 1930s

Manama Market in the 1950s

Cover of *Al-Ansar* Magazine, November 1944 (1363 Hijri)

Cover of *Al-Ansar* Magazine

Cover of *Sout Al-Bahrain* Magazine

Mr. Ahmed Sabri

My teacher, Ebrahim Alorayedh

Glimpses into the Biography of Taqi Muhammad Al-Baharna

*

* He was born in Bahrain, in the city of Manama, in 1930 A.D.
* He was educated in Bahraini and Iraqi schools.
* He studied literature, economics, and Arab and Islamic affairs. On his own.
* Participated in the activities of national, cultural, and social clubs.
* Engaged in self-employment and became a member of the boards of directors of a number of banks, insurance companies, chambers of commerce, and financial institutions.
* Owner of Taqi Muhammad Al-Baharna Trading Est.
*He held the positions of Bahrain's first Ambassador to Egypt and its permanent representative to the League of Arab States during the years 1971–1974.
* Member of the Shura Council and Chairman of the Foreign Affairs Committee 1993–2002.

* Vice President of the "Sheikh Isa Award for Service to Humanity."
* Participated in local and Arab cultural, social, literary, and economic conferences and seminars.
* Active member of the Arab Thought Forum—Amman, Jordan.
* Honorary President of the Education and Training Association—Bahrain.
* Member of the Board of Trustees of Abdul Rahman Kanoo International School.
* He was appointed by His Majesty, the King of Bahrain, to implement the national charter and was a member of the Charter Drafting Committee in 2002.
* Wrote articles and journals in the fields of poetry, literature, economics, and Arab and Islamic affairs in Bahraini newspapers and Arab magazines.
* He chronicled the biography of the Orouba Club throughout the years 1939–1990 and published it in a book in 1992.
* He has a book of poetry printed under the name "Banat Al-Sha'ar," which was published in 1996.
* He wrote his autobiography called, "Colored Papers," which was published in 1998.
* He authored a book of poetry called, "In My Mind, Crying Nostalgia," which was published in 2003.
* He has a third published book of poetry called, "Who Lights the Lamp," which was published in 2009.

* Author of the book, "Ahadiths and Biographies," which was published in 2010.

* He wrote a fourth book of poetry entitled, "At Dawn the Words Light Up," which was published in 2019.

* Author of the book, "Memoirs of an Ambassador" about his diplomatic activity as the Ambassador of Bahrain in the Arab Republic of Egypt 1971–1974 and was published in 2016.

* Author of the book, "My Travels and Memories," which was published in 2021.

* Recipient of the Certificate of Appreciation for Pioneers of Journalism by the Gulf Press Federation in 2010.

* Recipient of the Pioneers of Journalism Appreciation Award in Bahrain—Ministry of Information in 2008.

* Recipient of the State Appreciation Award for National Action from His Highness, the Prime Minister—Bahrain in 1992.

* Recipient of the Certificate of Appreciation for Diplomatic Work from the Ministry of Foreign Affairs of the State of Bahrain in 2009.

* Recipient of the First-Class Order of Merit from President Anwar Sadat in 1973.

* Recipient of the Sheikh Isa Medal of the First Degree by His Majesty, the King of Bahrain, in 2001.

* Recipient of the Order of Bahrain, First Class, from His Majesty, the King of Bahrain

* Recipient of the Gulf Cooperation Council Award for Excellence in Politics and Diplomacy in 2015.
* Evaluation of the Bahrain Commission for Inquiry recommendations regarding the political people's demands, as he was chosen to head the reconciliation team in 2011–2012.
* Active member of the Bahrain Red Crescent Society.